Franklin D. Roosevelt

IN THE SAME SERIES

General Editors: Eric J. Evans and P. D. King

LANCASTER PAMPHLETS

Franklin D. Roosevelt

The New Deal and War

M.J. Heale

London and New York

First published 1999
by Routledge
11 New Fetter Lane, London EC4P 4EE

Simultaneously published in the USA and Canada
by Routledge
29 West 35th Street, New York, NY 10001

Typeset in Bembo by Routledge
Printed and bound in Great Britain by Clays Ltd, St Ives plc

British Library Cataloguing in Publication Data
A catalogue record for this book is available from the British Library

Library of Congress Cataloging in Publication Data
Heale, M. J.
Franklin D. Roosevelt—the New Deal and war / Michael Heale.
p. cm.— (Lancaster pamphlets)
1. United States—Politics and government—1933–1945.
2. Roosevelt, Franklin D. (Franklin Delano), 1882–1945.
3. New Deal, 1933–1939. 4. World War, 1939–1945.
I. Title. II. Series.
E806.H43 1999
973.917—dc21   98.54315
                                                                CIP

ISBN 0–415–14588–0

Contents

Foreword

Lancaster Pamphlets offer concise and up-to-date accounts of major historical topics, primarily for the help of students preparing for Advanced Level examinations, though they should also be of value to those pursuing introductory courses in universities and other institutions of higher education. Without being all-embracing, their aims are to bring some of the central themes or problems confronting students and teachers into sharper focus than the textbook writer can hope to do; to provide the reader with the results of recent research which the textbook may not embody; and to stimulate thought about the whole interpretation of the topic under discussion.

Preface

This is a study of the most important American political figure of the twentieth century and of the United States over which he presided. Franklin D. Roosevelt was the only American to be elected president four times, and in his twelve years in the White House he personified the American response first to the Great Depression and then to the Second World War. The unparalleled crises that confronted the United States in the middle decades of the century touched virtually every American, and no president has borne greater responsibility than the lone figure in the wheelchair in the Oval Office. No other president, too, witnessed greater changes in the country around him.

Franklin Roosevelt's administration was a major watershed in American history. When he first took the oath of office in 1933 the United States was to a large extent a land of small-town values, minimal government, and isolation from the affairs of the world. This was the traditional America presided over by Anglo-Saxon and Protestant elites, the America of the Model T Ford, of Prohibition, of economic laissez-faire. By 1945 a new and modern America had taken shape, one characterised by metropolitan values, pervasive governmental bureaucracy and world power pretensions. This was the United States that would dominate the second half of the twentieth century: the America of the nuclear bomb, of assertive ethnic minorities, of power centred in Washington. Franklin D. Roosevelt, more than any other single person, gave direction to this fundamental transformation of American political society. Subsequent presidents have had to operate in his long shadow.

Acknowledgement

The maps 'The War in the Pacific, 1942–1945' and 'War in Europe and Africa, 1942–1945' are both from *The American Age: US Policy at Home and Abroad, Volume 2, Since 1896*, second edition, by Walter Lafeber. Copyright 1994 by W.W. Norton & Company, Inc. Reprinted by permission of W. W. Norton & Company, Inc.

Timechart

1882	January	Birth of Franklin Delano Roosevelt
1896	September	Roosevelt enters Groton School
1900	September	Roosevelt enters Harvard College
1905	March	Franklin Roosevelt marries distant cousin Eleanor Roosevelt
1907	June	Roosevelt joins Wall Street law firm
1910	November	Roosevelt elected to New York State Senate as Democrat
1912	November	Woodrow Wilson (Democrat) elected president
1913	March	Roosevelt appointed Assistant Secretary of the Navy
1917	April	United States enters First World War
1920	July	Democrats nominate James Cox for president and Roosevelt for vice-president
	November	Republicans under Warren Harding win presidential election
1921	August	Roosevelt crippled by poliomyelitis
1928	November	Election of Republican Herbert Hoover to the presidency
		Election of Franklin Roosevelt as Governor of New York
1929	March	Herbert Hoover inaugurated as president
	October 24	'Black Thursday': Stock market collapse
	October 29	Stock market prices fall 40 points

1930	June	Hawley-Smoot Tariff raises rates
	December	Congress authorises $100 million spending on public works
1931	August	New York's Temporary Emergency Relief Administration established
	September	United Kingdom comes off gold standard
1932	January	Reconstruction Finance Corporation (RFC) established
	July	Bonus Marchers driven from Washington
	November	Democrat Franklin D. Roosevelt defeats Herbert Hoover in presidential election
1933	March 4	Roosevelt inaugurated as president
	March 5	Roosevelt declares 4-day bank holiday
	March 9	Emergency Banking Act passed
	March–June	First 'hundred days'
	March 31	Civilian Conservation Corps (CCC) created
	April 19	USA comes off gold standard
	May 12	Federal Emergency Relief Administration (FERA) created
	May 12	Agricultural Adjustment Act creates Agricultural Adjustment Administration (AAA)
	May 18	Tennessee Valley Authority (TVA) created
	June 16	Glass-Steagall Banking Act
	June 16	National Industrial Recovery Act (NIRA) creates National Recovery Administration (NRA)
	June 16	Public Works Administration (PWA) established
	July	Roosevelt wrecks London International Economic Conference
	November 8	Civil Works Administration (CWA) established
	November 16	Roosevelt recognises Soviet Union
1934	April	Nye Committee of US Senate begins investigation of arms industry
	June 6	Securities Exchange Act creates Securities and Exchange Commission (SEC)
	June 12	Reciprocal Trade Agreements Act
	June 28	National Housing Act creates Federal Housing Administration (FHA)

	August	American Liberty League formed
	November	Democrats win large majorities in congressional midterm elections
1935	January 7	Supreme Court invalidates part of NIRA
	April	Works Progress Administration (WPA) created
	May	Rural Electrification Administration (REA) created
	May 27	'Black Monday': Supreme Court invalidates NIRA and other New Deal measures
	June	National Youth Administration (NYA) created
	July 5	National Labor Relations (Wagner) Act creates National Labor Relations Board (NLRB)
	August 14	Social Security Act
	August 23	Banking Act reconstitutes Federal Reserve Board
	August 26	Public Utility Holding Company Act
	August 30	Revenue Act
	August 31	Neutrality Act
	September 8	Senator Huey Long, leader of Share-Our-Wealth movement, assassinated
	October 3	Ethiopia invaded by Italy
	November 10	Committee (later Congress) of Industrial Organizations (CIO) formed
1936	January 6	Supreme Court invalidates Agricultural Adjustment Act
	February 29	Soil Conservation and Domestic Allotment Act
	March 7	Rhineland occupied by Germany
	July	Outbreak of Spanish Civil War
	August	Union party, organised by Father Coughlin, nominates William Lemke for president
	November 3	Roosevelt overwhelmingly defeats Republican Alfred Landon in presidential election; Democrats win large majorities in Congress
	December 29	Sit-down strike begins at General Motors (GM) plant at Flint
1937	February 3	Judiciary Reorganisation ('Court-packing') Bill submitted to Congress by Roosevelt

	February 11	GM capitulates to Union of Automobile Workers
	April 12	Supreme Court upholds National Labor Relations Act
	May 1	Neutrality Act, adds to neutrality legislation
	May 24	Supreme Court upholds Social Security Act
	July 22	Farm Tenancy Act creates Farm Security Administration
	September 1	Wagner-Steagall Housing Act creates United States Housing Authority
	October 5	Roosevelt's 'quarantine' speech
1938	February 16	Second Agricultural Adjustment Act
	March	Austria annexed by Germany
	June 16	Temporary National Economic Committee (TNEC) created
	June 25	Fair Labor Standards Act
	September	Munich Conference – UK and France agree to German occupation of Sudetenland
	November 8	Democrats lose congressional seats (though retain nominal majorities) in midterm elections
1939	March 15	Germany annexes remainder of Czechoslovakia
	April 3	Administrative Reorganization Act
	August	Nazi–Soviet Non-Aggression Pact
	September 1	Poland invaded by Germany
	September 3	United Kingdom and France declare war on Germany
	November 4	Neutrality legislation modified
	November 30	Finland invaded by Soviet Union
1940	April–June	Germany invades Norway, Denmark, Holland, Belgium, France
	May 10	Winston Churchill becomes Prime Minister of Great Britain
	May–June	British troops evacuated from Dunkirk
	June 29	Alien Registration (Smith) Act: aliens to register and sedition prohibited
	September	USA gives 50 destroyers to UK in return for naval bases
	September	Selective Service Act
	September	Battle of Britain begins

	September 22	Japan invades French Indo-China
	September 27	Axis–Japanese military pact
	November 5	Roosevelt re-elected president over Republican Wendell Willkie
1941	March 12	Lend–Lease Act
	June	Germany invades Soviet Union
	June 25	Roosevelt issues Executive Order 8802 banning racial discrimination in defence industries
	July	United States severs commercial relations with Japan
	August 15	Roosevelt and Churchill sign Atlantic Charter
	December 7	Pearl Harbor naval base attacked by Japan
	December 8	Congress declares war on Japan
	December 11	Germany and Italy declare war on United States
1942	January 1	United Nations declaration signed by 26 Allied nations
	January 12	War Labor Board created
	February 15	Japanese take Singapore
	February 19	Roosevelt issues Executive Order 9066 authorising internment of Japanese-Americans
	May	Japanese complete conquest of Philippines
	June	Battle of Midway
	August	Manhattan Project to build atomic bomb secretly begun
	October	Office of Economic Stabilization created under James F. Byrnes
	October 21	Revenue Act greatly widens tax base
	November 3	Republicans regain many seats (though not majorities) in midterm congressional elections
	November 8	Anglo-American forces land in North Africa
1943	January	Casablanca conference between Roosevelt and Churchill
	January 30	German armies surrender at Stalingrad
	February	Allied forces defeat Axis forces in North Africa
	June	Race riot in Detroit

	July	Allied forces land in Sicily
	September	Allied forces invade Italy
	September	Italian government withdraws from war
	November	Cairo conference between Roosevelt, Churchill and China's Chiang Kai-shek
	November	Tehran conference between Roosevelt, Churchill and Stalin
1944	February	Congress passes Revenue Act of 1944 over Roosevelt's veto
	June	Operation Overlord (Allied invasion of Normandy) launched
	June	Soviet offensive against Germany launched
	July	Bretton Woods conference, establishing International Monetary Fund and World Bank
	August–October	Dunbarton Oaks conference, planning creation of United Nations
	August	Paris liberated
	October	American forces begin liberation of the Philippines
	October	Battle for Leyte Gulf
	November 7	Roosevelt re-elected president over Republican Thomas E. Dewey
1945	February	Yalta conference between Roosevelt, Churchill and Stalin
	March	Anglo-American forces cross the Rhine
	April 12	Franklin D. Roosevelt dies; Harry S. Truman becomes president
	April–May	Soviet forces take Berlin
	April 28	Benito Mussolini killed
	April 30	Adolf Hitler commits suicide
	May 7	Germany surrenders
	July 16	Detonation of atomic bomb at Alamagordo, New Mexico
	July–August	Potsdam conference between representatives of USA, UK, USSR
	August 6	Atomic bomb dropped on Hiroshima
	August 8	Soviet Union joins war against Japan
	August 9	Atomic bomb dropped on Nagasaki
	August 10	Japan offers to surrender
	September 2	General MacArthur formally accepts Japanese surrender

WAR IN EUROPE AND AFRICA,
1942-1945

▓ Axis Powers at outbreak of war	
▨ Maximum extent of Axis military power	← Allied offensives
◢ Allies	– – – Heaviest Allied aerial bombing
☐ Neutral countries	········· Inside limit of German U-boat operations

Map 1

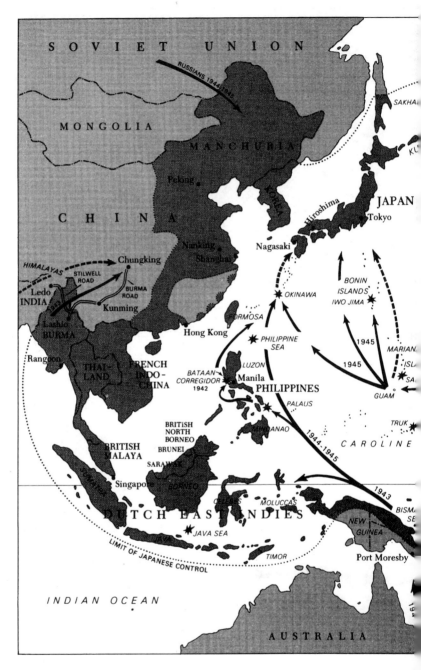

Map 2

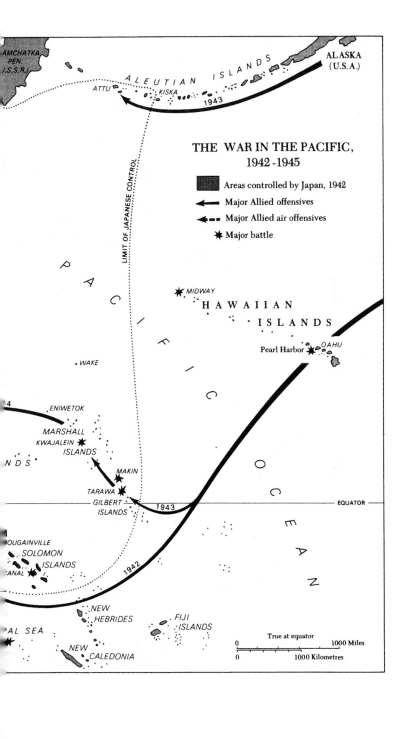

KAMCHATKA PEN. J.S.S.R.

ALASKA (U.S.A.)

ALEUTIAN ISLANDS

ATTU   KISKA   1943

LIMIT OF JAPANESE CONTROL

THE WAR IN THE PACIFIC, 1942 -1945

Areas controlled by Japan, 1942

Major Allied offensives

Major Allied air offensives

Major battle

P A C I F I C

O C E A N

MIDWAY

HAWAIIAN ISLANDS

Pearl Harbor   OAHU

WAKE

4

ENIWETOK

MARSHALL

KWAJALEIN

ISLANDS

MAKIN

TARAWA

GILBERT ISLANDS   1943   EQUATOR

N D S

BOUGAINVILLE

SOLOMON

ISLANDS

CANAL

1942

NEW HEBRIDES

FIJI ISLANDS

AL SEA

NEW CALEDONIA

True at equator

0   1000 Miles

0   1000 Kilometres

1

FDR, a man for all seasons

During his presidency Franklin Roosevelt provoked an extraordinary range of emotions. For many hungry Americans during the Depression he was the man doling out the provisions at the head of the breadline. 'Roosevelt is the only man we ever had in the White House who would understand that my boss is a sonofabitch', said one southern millworker. A Texas furniture worker echoed the sentiment: 'I will say...you are the one & only President that ever helped a Working Class of People.' 'If ever there was a Saint, He is one', thought a Wisconsin woman, 'as long as President Roosevelt will be our leader under Jesus Christ we feel no fear.' Northern Black Americans, who had traditionally voted Republican, returned a massive vote of confidence in Roosevelt in 1936 when, according to a Gallup Poll, a phenomenal 76 per cent voted for him. 'If he were in India today they would probably decide that he had become Mahatma', mused one Senator, '– that is, one in tune with the infinite'. A Republican politician despaired of the enthusiasm for Roosevelt felt by the people in his Philadelphia district: 'They seemed to think he gives you even the air you breathe and it would be a desecration to vote against him.'

The widespread affection and adulation for Roosevelt were balanced by powerful springs of hatred. A United States Senator publicly compared Roosevelt to the Beast of the Apocalypse, 'who set his slimy mark on everything'. To his extremist political opponent Charles Coughlin, Roosevelt was a 'betrayer', a 'liar', an 'upstart dictator', and even 'anti-God'. Among the letters which poured into the White House was one which told the president: 'If you were a good honest man, Jesus Christ would not have crippled you.' To many wealthy Americans he was a traitor to his class or, simply and unspeakably, 'that man'. The forces of organised money, cried Roosevelt in the 1936 campaign, 'are unanimous in their hate for me – and I welcome their hatred'. When the well-heeled commuters on a Lackawanna train heard of Roosevelt's sudden death in 1945, they cheered.

Probably no previous president, with the exception of Abraham Lincoln, had been the focus of quite such a powerful brew of emotions. For one thing, Roosevelt's capacity to arouse both love and hate among such large sections of the population testified to the growing importance of the presidential office. But Roosevelt's own personal history also helps to explain the intensity of public reactions to him, what he had been, what he represented, and what he had become.

FDR's roots were in the New York aristocracy, a group of landed families which had succeeded in passing status and wealth from generation to generation. The Roosevelts were of Dutch descent, a pedigree that linked them to the very origins of the colony, and Franklin, born in 1882, had been afforded an elite education at Groton School and at Harvard University. Theodore Roosevelt, President of the United States when Franklin was in his twenties, was a distant cousin, and Franklin had married another distant cousin, Eleanor Roosevelt. ('Well, Franklin, there's nothing like keeping the name in the family', Cousin Teddy had said when he gave away Eleanor at the wedding.) This background was more suggestive of a European style of patrician leadership than of the self-made qualities supposedly honoured in the United States. Like Theodore Roosevelt, the young Franklin had aligned himself with the progressive politics of the early twentieth century, although where Theodore was a Republican Franklin had made his own career in New York's Democratic party. In 1910 he was elected to the New York state senate, where he won a reputation as a reformer, early on engaging in combat with the bosses of Tammany Hall (the Democratic political machine in New York City). He joined Woodrow Wilson's administration in 1913 as Assistant Secretary of the Navy, which he energetically mobilised in 1917 when the United States was plunged into the First World War, and served as the Democrats' candidate for vice president in 1920, cheerfully if vainly stumping for progressive causes and the League of Nations.

Several months after that presidential election this ambitious young politician was subjected to an experience which was to change his life. His legs were paralysed by polio and he was never to walk unaided again. The effect of this trauma is incalculable, though it has been credited with weaning him off his patrician arrogance, and it perhaps served to reinforce the humanitarian instinct that Roosevelt had already shown. The experience may have helped him to meet later political crises with the robust confidence that was the marvel of his aides. He soon returned to Democratic politics and in 1928 was prevailed upon to run for the governorship of New York, a race in which Roosevelt distinguished himself by winning in defiance of the Republican landslide that swept Herbert Hoover into the White House. As governor, Roosevelt sustained his reformist stance as the economy collapsed, promoting the cause of conservation and pioneering state aid for the unemployed. When the Democrats searched for a winnable candidate for the 1932 presidential election, with the Republicans hopelessly compromised by the Great Crash and the Depression, Roosevelt's moment had come. As the scion of a famous political family, possessed of an ebullient personality, a rich oratorical talent, a progressive reputation as the governor of the largest state in the union, and even some affection from the South because of his summer home in Georgia, Roosevelt early emerged as the front runner. His nomination was secured when one of his rivals, John N. Garner of Texas, agreed to take the vice-presidential slot, following which Roosevelt dramatically broke with tradition by flying to Chicago to accept the nomination in person. 'Let it be from now on the task of our Party to break foolish traditions', he told the convention. 'I pledge you, I pledge myself, to a new deal for the American people.' Perhaps this was only a rhetorical flourish, but the media seized on the phrase and for contemporaries and later generations alike the Roosevelt administration became synonymous with the New Deal.

The precise meaning of the New Deal has been debated by scholars, but the Roosevelt administration (if not its reform programme) was to last twelve extraordinary years. In the election of 1932 Roosevelt carried 42 of the 48 states, aided by the unpopularity of the Republicans, the gloomy helplessness of Herbert Hoover, and his own capacity to radiate hope. The Democratic platform itself was cautious and Roosevelt's speeches were short on specifics, but the energetic Roosevelt campaign managed to project a sense that something could be done. The nature of the New Deal became clearer as the new administration grasped for ways of combating the Depression, although it was its very fearlessness that captured the admiration of many. The British socialist Harold Laski wrote in 1934 that 'compared with…the unimaginative activity of the British government', the New Deal was '…an exhilarating experiment'. Its various experiments were hardly unqualified successes, but a new burst of legislation in 1935 helped Roosevelt to an even greater electoral victory in 1936. Roosevelt carried every state in the Union save Maine and Vermont, and the Democrats won large majorities in both houses of

Congress. As it happened, this Democratic landslide did not produce another sustained period of reform, but by the end of the decade foreign crises were overshadowing domestic tribulations. War broke out in Europe in 1939, and the fearful possibility of American embroilment gave the popular Roosevelt an opportunity to run yet again in the 1940 election, the first time in American history that the tradition that presidents retire after two terms was defied. Perhaps in part because of this the exuberant businessman Wendell Willkie fared rather better than previous Republican candidates against Roosevelt, but FDR again demonstrated his ascendancy, with the assistance of strong support in the big cities. In 1944, with the United States at war, the electorate gave the Commander-in-Chief a similar margin of victory over his new Republican rival, the Governor of New York, Thomas E. Dewey. It was only Roosevelt's death in April 1945 that finally removed 'that man' from the White House.

Roosevelt owed his political longevity in large part to crisis. Both depression and war were of terrifying proportions. The whole future of American capitalism had been called into question when the banks were collapsing and a quarter of the labour force was out of work, while Hitler's astonishing success in conquering much of continental Europe in 1940, paralleled by Japanese expansionism in the Far East, promised a conflict of greater magnitude than even the sanguinary First World War. But a president who responded ineptly to crisis might not have been re-elected. President Hoover's helplessness in response to the Slump cast an unhappy shadow over the Republican party for many years, while Roosevelt's self-confidence and patent humanity in the face of both domestic and foreign crises served him and the Democrats well. Here was a president who seemed to feel some empathy with hungry and desperate Americans and with the victims of fascist aggression. His policies did not please all Americans, and he made his share of mistakes, but he showed that he was prepared to look for solutions and to use the powers at his disposal constructively. During these years Washington became a city of frenetic activity, and Roosevelt's command of his administration could not be doubted. If his enemies reviled him with a chilling bitterness, this was in part because his confidence and charisma early made him a president of massive stature. The poet Carl Sandburg in a radio broadcast in 1940 spoke of the president as 'a not perfect man and yet more precious than fine gold'.

To personal charm Roosevelt added a pragmatic temperament. While well-educated and possessed of a powerful curiosity, he was not an especially learned man and he avowed no sophisticated political philosophy, beyond a rather vague identification with progressive values. His campaign speeches in 1932 were hardly models of consistency, for he spoke both of cutting the federal budget and of spending more on the unemployed. During his presidency he exasperated his aides by patching together programmes that took elements from seemingly incompatible approaches. 'I always hate the frame of mind which talks about "your group" or "my group" among Liberals', said Roosevelt on one occasion. When asked how he would explain to people the political philosophy behind the Tennessee Valley Authority, he replied, 'I'll tell them it's neither fish nor fowl, but, whatever it is, it will taste awfully good to the people of the Tennessee Valley.' If he was not guided by a coherent ideology, he was guided by a belief in action and experimentation. The French premier Leon Blum wrote in 1936 that 'What has been most remarkable about the Roosevelt experiment has been the courage of President Roosevelt to try one method after another, to refuse to take a stubborn stand against experience, to try something else until at last he found the method that succeeded.' Improvisation could be said to be the central characteristic of the New Deal, as Roosevelt confusingly embraced and abandoned ideas and challenged his associates to devise yet more remedies. This open-mindedness was one of Roosevelt's strengths, as was the flexibility that allowed him to take advantage of any passing opportunity. Yet his was not a shallow opportunism. When he bent to the political winds it was with a view to enhancing rather than surrendering his leadership, to giving the nation a sense of direction. Domestically, he strove for greater economic security for American citizens and a more humane and accountable form of capitalism, and internationally he wanted the United States to play a role in promoting a peaceful and stable world.

Roosevelt's presidential stature was enhanced by his self-confidence. 'He must have been psychoanalysed by God', observed one contemporary. Playwright (and Roosevelt speechwriter) Robert Sherwood spoke of the president's 'heavily forested interior' and thought him 'spiritually the healthiest man I have ever known'. Unlike some presidents, Roosevelt was not in awe of grand heads of state, captains of industry, or distinguished intellectuals, nor ill at ease with ordinary folk. His patrician background and early personal crises seemed to bequeath him a serenity that allowed him to deal with people of all ranks with equanimity. This enabled Roosevelt both to stand up to pressure and to make use of a remarkable range and depth of talent. It may be doubted whether any other US administration of the twentieth century has been staffed at all levels with such a wealth of ability and skill. Roosevelt's affability also served him well in reaching the wider public. Reporters liked him, and the light banter of his frequent press conferences translated in the newspapers into a president in easy command of his job. His celebrated 'fireside chats' on the radio reached millions, as he used his aristocratic cadences to convey government policy in direct and homely terms. Roosevelt was the 'great communicator' of his generation, skilfully using the media to reach out directly to the people as no president had done before him.

This is not to suggest that Franklin Roosevelt was without fault. His instinctive pragmatism could mean that particular New Deal programmes were crippled by contradictory goals, and he was loath to admit mistakes. Many of his measures simply failed to accomplish their objectives or were harmful in their economic or social consequences. Roosevelt's flexibility was allied to a disregard for orderly procedures, and the lines of authority within his White House were far from clear. His charm endeared him to many, but officials and politicians were often infuriated by his ambiguous assurances. He could be difficult to pin down, and his evasiveness sometimes fed suspicions that differing messages were being conveyed to the shifting clusters of people and interests around him. The decisiveness that Harry Truman tried to display as president may have owed something to the prevarication that he had impatiently perceived in his predecessor. Still, ambiguity and evasiveness can be used to good effect by a consummate political operator.

FDR's political longevity, of course, was not merely the product of the interaction of political crises with his inimitable personality. The shock of depression and Roosevelt's skills also made it possible for him to build a durable political coalition. The Great Crash and Depression abruptly made the Democrats the majority party, the party that would win most presidential and congressional elections for a generation and more. But the New Deal helped to solidify the majority status that the Democrats had assumed in 1932. Roosevelt had never been an obedient servant of the Democratic party, taking on party bosses and wooing progressive Republicans when it served his interests. As president he was able to use his popularity in some measure to refashion the party, and central to this process was the forging of what is sometimes known as the New Deal coalition. By the mid-1930s this had taken reasonably precise form. One element was the urban working class, much of it of relatively recent immigrant stock. The nation's big cities had once been Republican strongholds but by the 1930s they had been claimed by the Democrats; in the elections of 1936, 1940 and 1944 they were to return large majorities for Roosevelt. Many urban political machines threw in their lot with the New Deal, whose programmes promised new sources of patronage, and organised labour also played its part in firming up the urban vote. In 1936 the newly formed Congress of Industrial Organisations (CIO), an alliance of industrial unions, was giving organisational support and generous funds to the Democrats, and industrial unionism was to remain a vital part of the New Deal coalition. Other constituencies too gave unprecedented support to the Democrats. African Americans, who had traditionally voted Republican where they had voted at all, shifted massively to the Democrats in the 1930s. Jews also gave Franklin Roosevelt their enthusiastic support. A few internationally-minded businessmen, like Averell Harriman, also lent their talents to the New Deal, and if they helped to curb its radical tendencies, so did a much more formidable bastion of political conservatism, the white South. The Democratic party had long enjoyed a near monopoly in the South, and southern Democrats had become the uneasy guardians of the tradition of white supremacy, a role which rendered many of them suspicious of progressive politics of any variety.

This coalition of urban labour, city machines, northern blacks, liberal intellectuals and white southern moderates and conservatives sat uneasily together, and eventually its tensions were to tear it apart. But that was decades into the future. In the New Deal years it was united in support of Franklin Roosevelt, and it repeatedly returned him to the White House, as it also ensured Democratic majorities in Congress and in many state governments. Some presidents had seen themselves as the agents of their party; for Roosevelt, the party was the agent of the president. The New Deal coalition was to survive Roosevelt's death and sustain the political power of the Democrats until the era of the Vietnam War. Given that it was built largely around the charismatic Roosevelt, it is perhaps surprising that it survived for so long.

Roosevelt was still under 60 when he was elected for a third term in 1940, however, and at that date few could imagine his demise. One story told in the next presidential campaign was of the fervent Democrat who responded to the remark that his newborn son could grow up to be president with the startled: 'Why? What's the matter with Roosevelt?' By that date Roosevelt's stature had been enhanced even further by the role that he was playing on the world stage. Where Adolf Hitler had come to personify Nazi Germany, Franklin Roosevelt was the personification of American democracy, submitting to yet another election in the midst of war. Even the British had suspended the electoral process while war raged, and alone among the major participants the American government continued to derive its legitimacy from an active (if not an equal) citizenry. In Britain, Winston Churchill, recalled from the wilderness, stamped an indelible mark on history by his wartime leadership, coming to stand for the bulldog determination of his island people to withstand Nazi aggression. The third major figure of the Grand Alliance was Marshal Joseph Stalin, the 'man of steel' whose control of the Soviet Union seemed absolute. In 1943 Roosevelt met with Churchill and Stalin at Tehran, and in 1944, as Hitler's monstrous empire was crumbling, the three met again at Yalta to try to settle the shape of the post-war world. No one loomed larger among these men of destiny than the President of the United States.

2

The slump

'I have no fears for the future of our country', said President Herbert Hoover in his Inaugural Address in March 1929, 'It is bright with hope.' In October share prices on the Stock Market spectacularly collapsed, declining on average by 40 per cent, but even that did not entirely destroy confidence in the world's leading economy. 'Things are better today than they were yesterday', said motor tycoon Henry Ford in November. But it was soon clear that a devastating depression was succeeding the Crash, one that hit Americans far harder than the people of any other industrial country. Over half of the drop in the world's industrial production occurred in the United States. 'The stock market crash', noted the writer Edmund Wilson, 'was to count for us almost like a rending of the earth in preparation for the Day of Judgment.'

In 1930 industrial production dropped by 17 per cent; in 1932 it was down to little more than half what it had been in 1929. In 1929 there had been virtually full employment (only about 3 per cent were not in work), but by 1933 the official unemployment figure was nearly 25 per cent, and the real number may have been even greater. If farm employees are excluded from the statistics, over a third of the country's workers were without jobs, a staggering figure in an industrial society. Even the possession of land did not mean security; one in eight farmers had lost his farm by 1933. The high and sustained level of unemployment in the United States overshadowed that of every other contemporary modern economy. And those lucky enough to be in work did not escape hardship; average weekly earnings fell from nearly $25 in 1929 to under $17 in 1932, and while prices fell too their fall was not as fast. Families raided their savings, fell into debt, and went hungry. And, in contrast to some other industrialised countries, the depression was nation-wide, devastating farm and city, east and west, the working and the middle classes, primary and consumer goods industries.

Unemployment brought fear and despair, for it could mean starvation and homelessness. The American suicide rate rose by nearly a quarter between 1929 and 1932, and there were instances of parents killing children that they could not feed. Marriage and birth rates dropped markedly, as young people recoiled from the prospect of raising families. Unlike the position in most western European countries, there were no welfare or dole payments for the unemployed to fall back on, except for the meagre relief sometimes available from local authorities. Only a tiny fraction – perhaps 2 or 3 per cent – of the millions of families without a male breadwinner received pensions. Private charity, the traditional American buffer against hard times and geared to limited and temporary distress, could not come close to meeting the scale of the emergency. In Chicago Al Capone opened the first breadline, perhaps hoping to recoup the popularity he had lost on St Valentine's Day 1929. Men roamed through the country looking for work, often drifting aimlessly or surreptitiously 'riding the rails'. In Washington State forest fires were started by men who hoped to be hired to put them out. Thousands of skilled workers sought jobs in the Soviet Union. African Americans learned anew that they were the 'first to be fired and the last to be hired', and Mexican Americans often reached a similar conclusion. Children scavenged garbage dumps and the refuse bins behind restaurants in search of food for their families. Countless Americans lost their savings and their homes. By 1933 about half of those who still clung to home mortgages were liable to eviction. People who had lost their homes slept in public parks, under bridges, even, in Arkansas, in caves. They sometimes took refuge in the shanty towns or 'Hoovervilles' that appeared outside large cities, living in packing cases and cardboard shacks. There were hunger marches and demonstrations in the early 1930s that sometimes produced modest improvements in particular communities, but they were difficult to sustain and many of the unemployed soon lapsed into a bitter apathy.

It was the hapless Herbert Hoover whose misfortune it was to preside over the United States in these years. Hoover, a Quaker, had been a very successful mining engineer and had entered public life during the First World War, when, in charge of food and relief efforts in Europe, he earned a considerable reputation as a humanitarian – he was sometimes known as 'the great humanitarian'. He nurtured an 'above politics' image, and members of both parties eyed him for the presidency in 1920. Born on a poor Iowa farm, Hoover's background was hardly patrician, but his energy and intelligence had secured for him a university education and a great fortune, and his aloof personality probably contributed to the grand image he came to possess. As a businessman he had believed in high wages and had displayed at least some sympathy for organised labour. In this he was in tune with the American progressive tradition, as he was in his emphasis on administrative efficiency, which he was again to display as Secretary of Commerce in the 1920s. In this office Hoover launched an assault on waste in business and used the resources of his department to analyse economic problems, point to solutions, and supply business with economic information. In his speech accepting the Republican presidential nomination in 1928, he even summoned his fellow citizens to a renewed assault on poverty: 'We in America today are nearer to the final triumph over poverty than ever before in the history of any land.' But if Hoover could betray progressive sentiments, he was a business progressive. By this date it had become clear that the humanitarian values he had revealed during the war came second to his belief in business efficiency, and at the time of his nomination for president he was identified with the conservative wing of the Republican party.

Hoover's organisational prowess and penetrating mind did not equip him sufficiently to deal with the misery that engulfed the country before his first year in office was over. The key to industrial recovery, he believed, was the restoration of business confidence, and he deployed his prodigious energy in exhorting businessmen and bankers to avoid deflationary actions (like reducing credit) and in stimulating private charities to feed the starving. These tactics had seemed to help the economy bounce back from recession in 1921, but the Great Depression proved more obdurate. Hoover called together business leaders to try to persuade them to limit wage reductions and lay-offs, but the number of jobless remorselessly grew. In 1930 Congress granted him money to spend on public works, but the funds were too small to have a measurable impact, Hoover was loath to add to the budget deficit, and state governments in any case cut their spending by even greater amounts. Hoover did authorise the government purchase of surplus wheat and cotton to arrest the catastrophic fall in farm income, but nothing was done to reduce production and the continued glut of these staples meant that their prices soon resumed their downward trend. In 1931 Hoover asked Congress to establish the Reconstruction Finance Corporation, which tried to shore up bank, railroad and other large companies by making loans to them. These key enterprises helped to sustain other businesses and a flow of credit, although it looked as if the administration was only interested in supporting big business. But in the event the loans were modest and the failure rate of business concerns reached a new high in 1932. In 1930 Hoover signed a new tariff act which raised protective tariffs to their highest level ever, sparking off retaliatory action by other countries that could only further depress international trade. In 1931 he agreed with fifteen other governments to suspend debt repayments between countries, but the level of international trade maintained its downward spiral and the depression continued to spread around the globe. A sharp increase in taxes in 1932, as Hoover tried to control the budget deficit, could only have a deflationary effect on the already devastated economy. Few of these measures directly addressed the plight of the unemployed, despite the evident failure of private charities and municipal governments to provide for them.

While these various measures represented some extension of the authority of the national government, many of them also depended for their success on the voluntary action of others – of state governments in maintaining spending, of farmers in reducing production, of employers in sustaining payrolls, of financiers in investing in private enterprise, of bankers in extending credit. When one leading businessman came up with a plan which would have allowed trade associations to enforce price and production levels and unemployment insurance on employers, Hoover denounced it as 'an attempt to smuggle fascism into America through the back-door'. One measure which illustrated his faith in voluntarism was the President's Emergency Committee for Employment, which spent its limited energies in exhorting state and local agencies to raise money for relief in their own communities. The federal government was to keep out of the relief business, which Hoover saw as a matter for private charities and local government, that is to say the traditional forms of community self-help. He believed there were dangers in allowing a bureaucratic state to take over people's lives (a perception for which he has since been congratulated by critics of big government). Hoover shrugged off the cascade of evidence that showed relief waiting lists growing ever longer, the resources of private agencies being depleted, local governments teetering towards bankruptcy, and the number of unemployed still insistently mounting.

Hoover was not heartless, but his rigid belief in self and local help and his sombre manner conveyed an impression of indifference. This impression was unhappily deepened when, as the 1932 election approached, some 20,000 veterans of the First World War marched on Washington to demand the payment of bonuses they believed due to them, and Hoover allowed the army to disperse these unarmed, ragged and hungry protesters with tanks and bayonets. Hoover, in short, failed to see that traditional and voluntarist methods could not cope with the scale of the destitution that characterised the Great Depression, and he and his party sacrificed the support of millions of Americans. It would be another twenty years before more than half the electorate could again be persuaded to cast their votes for a Republican candidate for president, and even then they did so only because that candidate (Dwight D. Eisenhower) was a war hero.

The Hoover administration was hampered both by the conventional wisdom of the day and by the limited instruments at the government's disposal for managing the economy and implementing social policy. Most professional economists believed in balanced budgets – state and national governments should not spend more than they received in revenue, otherwise business confidence would be undermined and inflation would result. Laissez-faire economists insisted that government interference could only intensify the problem of recovering from a depression, arguing that market forces had to reach a natural balance before an economy could spring back to full health. Hoover was not a doctrinaire advocate of laissez-faire, but he did accept the need to balance the federal budget, in so far as that was possible in such unpredictable times. Hence his decision for a tax increase as the budget lurched towards a large deficit in the later part of his term. By emphasising fiscal prudence, the conventional wisdom thus discountenanced notions that the American government might spend its way out of the Depression, relieve misery by handing out relief payments or create jobs through public works.

But even if Herbert Hoover had been an early convert to Keynesian economics, and even supposing that the doubts of a conservative Congress could have been overcome, it is unlikely that his administration could have devised effective measures to end the Depression. The federal government at this time was a flimsy edifice. By European standards, it could almost be said, the United States did not possess a central government. The veteran American diplomat George Kennan once recalled of his early boyhood days in the Midwest that, 'when times were hard, as they often were, groans and lamentations went up to God, but never to Washington'. There was no national education system, no national police force, not much in the way of a federal bureaucracy, and only a few people paid federal income tax. The routine tasks of governance were performed by local and especially state governments. The only federal agency in most towns was the post office. In 1929 federal expenditure represented a tiny 2.5 per cent of GNP and was only a third of that of state and local governments. An increase of federal spending of 50 per cent would have seemed massive to the Treasury but of itself would have sent no more than a slight ripple through the national economy. There was no government bank, and the national administration had no control over the monetary authorities, most notably the independent Federal Reserve Board which supervised the system of private banking (although the president appointed members to it). If Hoover had somehow contrived to decree unemployment or welfare payments, there was no government department through which to channel them and no system of local social security offices to administer them. When Hoover did agree to release surplus wheat to feed the hungry in 1932, it had to be distributed by the Red Cross. The absence of anything like the state welfare systems that were emerging in Europe meant that any attempts at social policy would be severely circumscribed. The tradition whereby communities looked after their own distressed residents had been the product of an agricultural society, when hardship could be expected to be local and temporary. The administrative structure of the federal government had simply not been adapted to the needs of an urbanised and industrialised nation.

By 1932 not only had Hoover's measures patently failed to produce recovery, but the economy was sinking even deeper into depression. The biggest drop in GNP in a single year occurred between 1931 and 1932, and in the same period unemployment rocketed by about 50 per cent. As the election of 1932 approached, there were some twelve million Americans miserably seeking work, an awesome figure which did not have its like in living memory. There were rumbles of discontent across the country, but no organised revolt against the American economic and political system. Many of the destitute were simply worn out from years of struggle. But perhaps, too, the American political process offered a measure of hope. The Depression was irretrievably identified with Herbert Hoover and the Republicans. Perhaps a change of government could offer a solution.

The Roosevelt campaign of 1932 was itself notably lacking in revolutionary promise. The platform followed conventional wisdom in speaking of the need for balancing the federal budget, and Roosevelt himself from time to time reiterated this demand. But his campaign was invested with an optimism that his gloomy rival could not match, and his pragmatism kept bursting through. Roosevelt spoke of 'distributing wealth and products more equitably, of adapting existing economic organization to the service of the people'. The means to this egalitarian end were not entirely clear, but Roosevelt seemed to be glimpsing a more positive role for government. Where major businesses abused their power, he suggested, the state might step in. What the campaign did reveal was Roosevelt's energy, determination and optimism in the face of national adversity. His coast-to-coast offensive effectively buried the image of a crippled body, and his skilful radio talks sent a note of hope into the furthest reaches of a devastated nation. His crushing victory marked the end of Republican hegemony.

Franklin Roosevelt won the election with over 57 per cent of the popular vote, the largest majority his party had ever enjoyed, and an even greater proportion of electoral votes. Hoover indeed carried only four New England states and but two others; Roosevelt took the rest. The Democrats' electoral success was confirmed by the congressional returns. They won a huge majority in the House of Representatives and a large one in the Senate. For the next thirty-odd years the Democrats were to be the majority party. During the inaugural parade the bands played 'Happy Days Are Here Again'. By this date the term 'New Deal' had entered the language, but it was far from clear what this meant or just how Americans could expect to exercise their inalienable right to the pursuit of happiness. Roosevelt may have intimated that they could expect more action from Washington, but as yet the structure of government remained as frail as ever.

3

Origins of the New Deal

'Our greatest primary task is to put people to work', said Franklin Roosevelt with understated simplicity at his inauguration in March 1933. The New Deal at this point was nothing like a thought-out programme, but Roosevelt's determination to do something shone through his modest rhetoric. 'I favor as a practical policy', he added, 'the putting of first things first'. This pragmatic humanitarianism was to sustain the New Deal through its philosophical twists and turns in the months and years ahead. His speech was broadcast across the nation, and close to half-a-million letters promptly flooded into the White House. 'Your human feeling for all of us in your address is just wonderful', said one.

The president's own advisers argued over the shape of the New Deal, but what they did agree on as the administration took shape was that the main causes of the Depression were internal. Latterly Hoover had been emphasising external causes, such as the decline in foreign markets for American goods, an analysis that suggested the inherent soundness of the American economy and the limited capacity of the federal government to put things right. In contrast Roosevelt's advisers insisted that the Depression was primarily domestic in origin, notably in the inadequacy of consumer purchasing power (itself in part the product of the failure of business during the good times to pass on productivity gains in higher wages or lower prices). Their analyses focused on structural and institutional weaknesses within the American economy, and while these weaknesses were not easily remedied, at least this approach implied that government could make a difference.

When President Roosevelt wheeled into the Oval Office on 5 March 1933 the economic crisis was at its most terrifying. The number of people officially unemployed now stood at a quarter of the workforce, and in many cities the proportion was far higher. 'I see on streets filthy, ragged, desperate-looking men, such as I have never seen before', a Washington resident had recently written. Many of those in work were barely eking a living in part-time jobs. US Steel remained a giant corporation, but by the time Roosevelt was settling into the presidency all its workers were part-time. Economic experts might disagree on who or what was responsible for this misery, but for many people bankers and big businessmen were deeply implicated. In gauging 'The Temper of the People', journalist George Sokolsky concluded: 'No banker, no great industrialist, no college president commands the respect of the American people.' By this date the spectacular incompetence of America's bankers was being demonstrated daily.

Through the winter of 1932–33 the primary symbols of American capitalism, the nations' banks, had been toppling like a row of dominoes, and state governors moved to stem the disaster by calling bank holidays. By March three-quarters of the banks had closed their doors, and European governments were rapidly removing money from American vaults. Hours before Roosevelt took the oath of office even the great financial states of New York and Illinois had suspended banking, and the New York and Chicago stock exchanges were closed. The collapse of the banking system threatened to bring business to a juddering halt. American capitalism seemed on the unimaginable verge of being turned into a barter economy. To columnist Arthur Krock the mood in Washington resembled that 'in a beleaguered capital in war time'.

Roosevelt's reaction to the banking crisis illustrated something of the New Deal. It was at once speedy, dramatic, constitutional and conservative. He did not seize dictatorial powers or seek to nationalise the banks, as some thought he might. On 5 March, his first full day in office, he proclaimed a national bank holiday. This bought him a few precious days in which to prepare legislation, and on 9 March he sent Congress his banking bill. Within less than eight hours it had been whisked through all the stages of that usually cumbersome body and had received the presidential signature. Three days later, on a Sunday evening, Roosevelt spoke to the nation in his first radio 'fireside chat', reassuring citizens that their money was now safe, and the next day the major banks opened their doors for business. Deposits flowed into the banks once more and the immediate crisis was over. Soon most banks were functioning again. It took a disgruntled Herbert Hoover to describe Roosevelt's declaration bank holiday as 'the American equivalent of the burning of the Reichstag to create "an emergency" '.

The Emergency Banking Act was fashioned largely by members of the banking community, and it reinstated rather than reformed the existing system, providing for the inspection of banks, supplying capital where necessary for the hard-pressed (through Hoover's Reconstruction Finance Corporation), and giving the president the authority to reopen banks when they showed themselves sound. But the president had pulled off his first coup: by speedy action, conservative means and a reassuring manner, he had restored confidence in the nation's banks.

Such qualities characterised much of the New Deal as it unfolded. Washington became the centre of frenetic activity. Young men (only a few women) poured into the city to participate in the exciting task of rebuilding the nation. Between 1933 and 1938 bill after bill poured out of the Roosevelt administration, and many of them made it into law. Few aspects of the nation's life remained untouched. Yet, exciting and innovative as these times were, they were hardly revolutionary. The degree of energy in Washington was unprecedented, but many of the measures, seen singly, were cautious in design.

These characteristics became apparent during Roosevelt's celebrated 'first hundred days' in office. Hoover had worked tirelessly to find solutions for the economic crisis, but his administration seemed inert in contrast to the blitzkrieg that followed. One break with the immediate past came with the repeal of Prohibition; at least Americans could take refuge in drink. Many of the measures of the first hundred days were necessarily emergency measures, hastily patched together, and as such it is hardly surprising that some were to fall foul of the Supreme Court. Roosevelt had asked Congress for broad powers to wage war against the emergency, and Congress obliged. In the spring and early summer of 1933 Roosevelt made fifteen major proposals, all of which Congress adopted. This Congress, it has been said with a little exaggeration, 'did not so much debate the bills it passed...as salute them as they went sailing by'.

When Roosevelt took office, about a quarter of the labour force was unemployed; together with their dependants, perhaps 50 million people were in desperate poverty. Among the measures of 1933 were the first-ever federal government attempts to offer a hand to the unemployed. Before the end of Roosevelt's first month in office an act had established the Civilian Conservation Corps (CCC), to provide work for young men in a range of tasks such as planting trees (millions of them), building forest trails and camp grounds, controlling mosquitoes and fighting forest fires. By the summer an extraordinary peacetime mobilisation had taken place, some 300,000 men having been enlisted in this 'forestry army'. Over 2.5 million youngsters were eventually to participate in this most popular of New Deal programmes.

A little later came the Federal Emergency Relief Administration (FERA), under the energetic Harry Hopkins, to provide 'sufficient relief to prevent physical suffering and to maintain living standards'. Within his first two hours in the job Hopkins had spent over $5 million. His task, he said, was 'to feed the hungry and Goddam fast'. The FERA made direct grants to the needy, although it preferred to disburse money to state and local governments to fund public projects, sometimes on a matching funds basis (which meant that relief payments varied enormously from state to state). Its dedicated officials probed the nature of poverty imaginatively and tested new strategies for addressing it. By the time that it closed in December 1935 the FERA had spent about $4 billion, mostly federal money, although even this unprecedented amount seemed puny given the scale of the problem. But the FERA had saved many a family from starvation, and, although only intended as a temporary emergency measure, it represented a kind of revolution – it had decisively broken the federal government's tradition of staying out of relief work.

Another tradition was overturned with the decision to provide governmental support for farmers. It was the crisis in agriculture that early riveted the attention of New Deal officials. Over 40 per cent of the population lived in rural areas, and in places the threat of violence simmered. In a sense farmers were simply producing too much. Overproduction followed by the collapse of markets both at home and abroad during the Depression had meant precipitate drops in farm prices, unnerving farm indebtedness, and countless foreclosures. Total farm income in 1932 was less than half what it had been in 1929. In the Midwest farmers were threatening a national farm strike – withholding goods from market. A quarter of Mississippi's land was auctioned off in one day as farmers went under. Once the banking crisis had been surmounted, the administration turned to the farms. The result was the Agricultural Adjustment Act, setting up the Agricultural Adjustment Administration (AAA).

The basic strategy of the AAA programmes was to try to increase farm prices by reducing production. The carrot would be subsidies for cooperative farmers, who would be paid to reduce the acreage farmed in a given year. By such means farm prices might be returned to 'parity' with those enjoyed in the good years before the First World War; the government was undertaking to maintain the purchasing power of farmers at a relatively generous level. The programmes required the participation of farmers themselves to help set quotas and administer production controls for each commodity, a feature that tended to work to the advantage of the larger farmers who often sat on local committees. Farmers in effect were being encouraged to behave much as industrial corporations, securing greater control over output and prices. Some chose to remain outside the schemes.

Because the act went into operation after some foodstuffs like corn and pork were already in production for 1933, the yield could be reduced only by destroying the products, and at a time when many Americans were going hungry the AAA was obliged to slaughter 8.5 million piglets. Such desperate measures were not repeated, but the image of the AAA was hardly enhanced. Joseph Heller caricatured the AAA in *Catch 22*, where he recalled of a farmer in the 1930s: 'The government paid him for every bushel of alfalfa he did not grow. The more alfalfa he did not grow, the more money the government gave him, and he spent every penny he didn't earn on new land to increase the amount of alfalfa he did not produce.' Farm prices were soon to rise again, although it is unclear how far the production controls themselves were responsible. Perhaps more helpful to farmers was the credit made available by New Deal programmes. Late in 1933 the Commodity Credit Corporation was established to provide loans on stored crops like cotton and corn; only if prices rose above a given level would the loans have to be repaid. So was born the celebrated price-support system which would provide for farm stability for the next half-century. The New Deal's agricultural policies met with some success, so that by 1936 farm incomes were increasing.

It would have been difficult successfully to raise farm and other prices without devaluation of the dollar, and to effect this Roosevelt took the United States off the gold standard as the agriculture bill was being considered. 'Well, this is the end of Western civilisation', concluded an appalled Director of the Budget. Roosevelt seemed more amused than alarmed by such imprecations, and as it happened civilisation did not fall, but prices did rise somewhat, providing a little assistance to farmers and business. The measure illustrated that Roosevelt was not in thrall to the conventional wisdom, as it also illustrated the economic nationalism of the early New Deal. If the New Dealers were right that the depression was largely the result of internal causes, they wanted to be free of international constraints to combat it. The same attitude prevailed in July when Roosevelt pulled the United States out of the International Economic Conference, which was then meeting in London to try to stabilise world currencies, thereby wrecking it. He did not wish to imperil his attempts to raise prices in the United States by premature currency stabilisation. He mocked the 'old fetishes of so-called international bankers' and welcomed their replacement 'by efforts to plan national currencies'. Before the end of his presidency he was to take a less insular view.

A month after enacting the AAA, Congress passed the National Industrial Recovery Act (NIRA), often seen as the centrepiece of the first hundred days. Again the economics of scarcity were employed in an effort to stabilise industry. The problem was assumed to be too much competition, which drove down prices and therefore wages and jobs, and the remedy a kind of regulated monopoly. Businessmen were to be protected from the anti-trust laws if, within each industry, they drew up 'codes of fair competition' governing prices, wages and production quotas. In short, businessmen were virtually being invited to set prices that might give them a reasonable return, thus avoiding overproduction and bankruptcies and sustaining employment. The aim, in the words of the administrator of the programme, was to get rid of 'eye-gouging and knee-groining and ear-chewing in business'. A morsel was offered to labour by Section 7a, which guaranteed the right to collective bargaining.

The National Recovery Administration (NRA) was set up under General Hugh Johnson to administer the codes. This was an attempt at co-operation between government and industry, though the marriage was to prove unhappy. Johnson's energy was at first impressive, and by the autumn most major companies had endorsed wages and hours agreements. Curbs were placed on sweatshop conditions and the exploitation of child labour. But the codes were not easily enforced and the NRA was soon beset with squabbles. Small businesses resented the way in which big business dominated the code-writing process; most big firms detested the concessions afforded to labour; unions came to feel cheated of the protection they thought they had been promised; government grew weary of the wrangles and was disillusioned by the failure of the economy to recover more than marginally. The NRA helped to prop up manufacturing industry at a time when it needed support and some prices were stabilised, but it did not deliver industrial recovery.

In part the economic failure was government's responsibility. The act had also established the Public Works Administration (PWA) with a budget of $3.3 billion, and it was hoped that pump-priming via the funding of public works would do something to boost purchasing power. But, unlike Harry Hopkins and Hugh Johnson who tried to introduce their programmes with furious speed, the old Progressive Harold Ickes was determined on giving the taxpayer value for money and insisted on rigorous appraisals before approving public works projects. Eventually the PWA would be responsible for many valuable public projects like bridges, tunnels, courthouses, hospitals and school-buildings. But the money was injected too slowly to give the economy much of a boost and in May 1935, when the Supreme Court struck down the NRA, industrial production was only a little greater than it had been in June 1933.

More successful was another celebrated product of the hundred days, the Tennessee Valley Authority (TVA), established in May 1933 to develop one of the poorest regions in the United States, some 40,000 square miles reaching into seven states. Previous attempts to harness the power of the Tennessee River had been frustrated by conservative opposition and private power interests but, remarkably, the TVA was empowered to construct and manage dams, generate cheap electricity, control flooding, prevent soil erosion and even produce nitrogen fertilisers for sale. The degree to which this public agency competed with private interests and worked with rural co-operatives provoked hostility from business conservatives, but it was to play a massive role in the economic development of several south-eastern states, particularly through the generation of electric power. In 1933 only 2 per cent of Tennessee Valley farms had electricity; by 1945 some 75 per cent did so.

There were other measures of the first hundred days, among them an act to protect homeowners from mortgage foreclosures and the Glass-Steagall Act to reform the banking system (among other things it boosted customers' confidence in banks by guaranteeing their deposits). Yet despite the frenetic activity, recovery did not follow swiftly. As the winter of 1933–34 loomed, Roosevelt secured another emergency measure, the Civil Works Administration (CWA), to provide work relief for the needy, exceptionally without a means test. This was to be better funded during its few months of life than the FERA, whose work it complemented, and it was also headed by Harry Hopkins. By February 1934 the various relief agencies – the FERA, the CCC and the CWA – were reaching over a fifth of the American population, an extraordinary figure. There were counties in which over half of the residents were on relief. Yet millions were denied relief and those that were favoured could not easily survive on relief alone.

The emergency measures of the spring and summer of 1933 helped to arrest the unnerving collapse of economic activity that seemed to be occurring in Herbert Hoover's last months in office. The principal economic indicators ceased to turn down, and by the end of Roosevelt's first year were looking a little stronger. Average earnings for workers and corporate receipts were moving up, farm-mortgage debt was declining, and the number of business failures was down. But real economic recovery proved frustratingly elusive. There was more legislation passed in 1934, including the Securities Exchange Act to curb stock market abuses, which put the stock exchanges under the supervision of the Securities and Exchange Commission (SEC). This was an important step in opening up the ways of American finance capitalists to scrutiny; Wall Street was to be regulated by Washington. Another measure of long-term significance was the Trade Agreements Act to promote the reduction of tariffs on a reciprocal basis. But these acts had little immediate effect on the economy. Extraordinary and unprecedented though the measures of the early New Deal were, by June 1934 there were still 11 million people unemployed.

The continued malaise exposed the New Deal to criticism from both left and right. A new Farmer-Labor Political Federation called for greater government action to raise wages and farm incomes, and encouraged third-party movements in a number of mid-western and western states. The Louisiana Senator Huey Long launched his Share-Our-Wealth campaign, urging a dramatic redistribution of income from rich to poor. On the right, some corporate conservatives and disgruntled Democrats took refuge in the American Liberty League, dedicated to the preservation of free enterprise. Despite such restiveness, however, Roosevelt's personal popularity with much of the electorate remained high while the Republicans remained deeply distrusted. The Democrats increased their majorities in both houses of Congress in the midterm elections of November 1934.

But the criticism of the administration was having an effect. Some of those elected to Congress in 1934 were more radical than the president, and the new Congress proved difficult to work with, balking at some of Roosevelt's proposals or amending them in ways uncongenial to the president. Harold Ickes thought Roosevelt 'distinctly dispirited': 'He looked tired and he seemed to lack fighting vigor or the buoyancy that has always characterized him.' The central measures of the hundred days of 1933 had not greatly stimulated the economy, and early in 1935 Roosevelt seemed uncertain what do next.

Occasional measures did pass Congress. Roosevelt had never been happy about simply doling out relief, and the continued high unemployment and the growing numbers on the welfare rolls induced him to think about work relief, that is giving jobs to the needy. A bill passed in May 1935 appropriated an extraordinary $4.54 billion and allowed him to set up the Works Progress Administration (WPA), again under Harry Hopkins (although the money was shared among a number of agencies). This would employ people rather than handing them a dole, and according to Roosevelt the work would be 'useful…in the sense that it affords permanent improvements in living conditions or that it creates future new wealth for the nation'. The WPA survived until 1943, during which time its various critics from all parts of the political spectrum exposed its many shortcomings. It was able to reach only about a third of the unemployed at any one time; it paid more than the FERA but less than the average private wage; and, in part because it was prohibited from competing with private industry, many of its projects seemed to invent work. Writer John Steinbeck was assigned the task of taking a census of the dogs on the Monterey Peninsula.

Nonetheless the WPA stands as an imaginative emblem of the New Deal. It was under the WPA that the Federal Theatre Project flourished, staging countless theatrical productions across the country and employing thousands of directors and actors, including John Huston and Orson Welles. Similarly, the Federal Writers' Project and the Federal Art Project found work for other talented (and untalented) intellectuals and artists, among them Saul Bellow, Richard Wright and Jackson Pollock. Lasting memorials of the New Deal are to be found on those public buildings still adorned by works of art. This was a remarkable phenomenon, the federal government supporting culture and trying to make it accessible to the public. 'Nowhere in Europe is there anything to compare with this', marvelled the Austrian composer Erich Wolfgang Korngold. Most WPA workers, though, found themselves employed in construction and other humdrum jobs. Associated with the WPA, too, was the National Youth Administration, which found part-time jobs for over 2 million students (among them Arthur Miller and Richard Nixon) and work for another 2.5 million unemployed young people. Altogether, the WPA was responsible for over a quarter of a million projects, such as the building or upgrading of highways, playgrounds, parks, zoos, schools, hospitals, military bases, airfields and even aircraft carriers. Not the least of its accomplishments was the provision of hot lunches for many schoolchildren. Broadly, the WPA won the imagination of liberals and intellectuals and the hostility of conservatives.

Also in May 1935 Roosevelt established the Rural Electrification Administration. At this point, some 90 per cent of American farms had no electricity, a luxury enjoyed by city folk. Over the next few years, in part through the formation of co-operatives, this potent form of energy was carried into the countryside, suddenly consigning to the past many of the wearisome and centuries-old routines of rural life. By 1941 electrification of farms had risen to 40 per cent, a steep climb which continued into the following decades. Probably no other single measure of the New Deal was as responsible for transforming life in the American South.

The innovations of the New Deal had been criticised from the beginning, but its conspicuous weaknesses by 1934–35 were giving its enemies some credibility. On the right the American Liberty League subjected the New Deal to sustained attack for its alleged socialistic proclivities. On the left some segments of organised labour voiced their disappointment, particularly with the NRA or 'National Run-Around'. More unsettling were the large followings being won by a number of populistic figures offering panaceas of their own. There was the elderly Californian doctor, Francis E. Townsend, whose proposal to give everyone over 60 a pension of $200 a month provided it were spent within the month, won millions of supporters, particularly among those over 60. The popularity of the Townsend Plan helped to concentrate administration minds on the issue of what should be done for the elderly. Even better known was Father Charles E. Coughlin, the celebrated 'radio priest', who was speaking to the largest regular radio audience in the world in 1934 and in the following year was mixing denunciations of Roosevelt with intimations of anti-Semitism. But the most formidable opponent of the New Deal was Senator Huey Long, the so-called 'Kingfish' of Louisiana, the effective ruler of the state and the leader of the Share-Our-Wealth campaign. By 1935 Long was claiming a membership of 8 million in his Share-Our-Wealth clubs and was demonstrating a remarkable popularity in the Plains states; one poll suggested that he might win 100,000 votes even in the supposedly sophisticated state of New York if he ran on a third-party ticket in 1936.

The New Deal was also meeting resistance from a more august quarter. Roosevelt's advisers had always feared that the remarkable extension of governmental activity launched by the New Deal might meet the disapproval of the United States Supreme Court, with its traditional protection of laissez-faire. Further, the haste with which emergency legislation had been thrown together rendered much of it vulnerable to judicial review. In the early months of 1935 the Supreme Court emerged as a major obstacle to the New Deal. In particular it took exception to what it saw as the New Deal's tendency to delegate legislative power to executive agencies, thus breaching the principle of the separation of powers. A section of the National Industrial Recovery Act concerning controls on interstate oil shipments was shot down in January; in May, in the so-called 'sick chicken' case, the Court unanimously annulled the entire act, thus destroying the NRA. On that 'Black Monday' it also invalidated a number of other New Deal measures.

A premise of the 'sick chicken' decision was that the power granted by the Constitution to Congress to regulate commerce could not be construed to mean that it could also regulate manufacturing. Such a narrow definition of the commerce clause threatened the New Deal's whole attempt to manipulate the economy. Franklin Roosevelt expostulated that the country had been 'relegated to the horse-and-buggy definition of inter-state commerce'. Congressman David J. Lewis demanded the curtailment of the authority of the Supreme Court because it had left Congress 'alone among parliaments, stripped of power to defend the nation against an economic depression more devastating than ordinary war'. By this date Roosevelt's attempts to work with the business community were also falling on barren ground. In late April the long-standing business suspicion of the New Deal broke through at the annual convention of the US Chamber of Commerce, which sweepingly denounced the New Deal programme. In the late spring of 1935 some observers believed the New Deal to be dead in the water.

4

Heyday of the New Deal

The early months of 1935 had not been happy ones for Franklin Roosevelt's administration. While some significant measures were secured, Roosevelt did not seem to be offering a clear sense of direction. For a time he tried to maintain an uneasy coalition of conservative and liberal interests, but his attempts to preserve business support met with little success while exposing him to attacks from radicals. Despite the apparent endorsement of the New Deal in the midterm elections of 1934, the critics on both left and right had remained unrelenting, and Congress had proved a somewhat unreliable friend of the administration. The US Chamber of Commerce exposed the depth of business ingratitude towards the New Deal in April, and the Supreme Court consummated a series of destructive decisions on 'Black Monday', 27 May, holing the New Deal vessel beneath the waterline. What was Franklin Roosevelt to do to save it?

The economy remained mired in depression. The employment figures had improved a little since the dark days of 1933, but only a little. About 20 per cent of the workforce was still unemployed. Finally, in June 1935, as Congress was about to wind up, Roosevelt hurled himself into action once more, demanding that Congress enact five major measures. In the unpleasantly hot summer months of 1935 congressmen stayed on in Washington to address themselves to the president's requests, and in this 'second hundred days' Congress enacted some of the most far-reaching laws in its history. These momentous measures placed Roosevelt closer to the liberals and radicals and revealed his exasperation with the business community.

This new burst of legislation has led some scholars to distinguish between a 'first New Deal', centred on the hundred days of 1933, and a 'second New Deal' launched in the 'second hundred days' of 1935, and to argue that the Roosevelt administration changed direction. Arthur Schlesinger has discerned a movement from left to right, as the Roosevelt administration abandoned its early attempts at economic planning and returned to trust-busting and the promotion of competition. Defined in terms of economic theory, this view has logic, but it exaggerates the degree of planning in the early New Deal and the seriousness of the assault on big business in the later part of it. More often, scholars have suggested that there was a swing from right to left, as the administration gave up its attempt to work with the business community and sought allies in the labour movement and among the lower classes. This approach also has some plausibility, but distinguishing between a 'first' and a 'second' New Deal at all obscures more than it illuminates. In assuming that there were carefully formulated programmes, it exaggerates the coherence of the New Deal at any one time; the Roosevelt administration was never governed by a single political ideology, and its components were always pulling in different directions. Many of the measures of the first hundred days were necessarily emergency measures, while those of 1935 tended to be the products of longer-term planning, some having evolved during the 'first' New Deal. They do not necessarily represent a change of heart on Roosevelt's part. But, in conventional terminology, it is true that from 1935 the New Deal was closer to the political left in that it stumbled into a somewhat uneasy alliance with organised labour and showed a greater interest in social reform.

One pivotal measure was the National Labor Relations Act, or the Wagner Act, passed in July 1935. Roosevelt himself, betraying an old Progressive's unease about organised labour, initially had not favoured this attempt to intervene in industrial relations, and it was largely the creation of the New York Senator Robert Wagner, working with labour economists and other Washington bureaucrats. But the Supreme Court had struck down the NIRA, including the attempt to protect the unions in Section 7a, thus throwing the administration's industrial strategy into disarray. At this juncture Roosevelt cast his weight behind Wagner's bill, ensuring its speedy passage. Collective bargaining was guaranteed, employers were to be prohibited from indulging in 'unfair labor practices', and the new system was to be overseen by an autonomous body, the National Labor Relations Board (NLRB). Thus began the New Deal's historic identification with organised labour. More than was the case in many other countries, the national government was getting into the business of regulating industrial relations. The state was inserting itself into a domain that employers had long considered to be theirs, and it was doing so more of its own volition than at the behest of labour.

Robert Wagner's objective was both to strengthen organised labour and to promote a healthier economy. He wanted fewer labour disputes, not more. The Wagner Act was based on the premise that collective bargaining could avert strikes and other forms of industrial disruption. Company unions and various forms of unfair employer practice were banned, and workers' rights were strengthened. The NLRB, for example, could order the reinstatement of an unfairly dismissed worker. Most important, workers could themselves choose which union would represent them exclusively, in elections administered by the NLRB. Employers would be obliged to recognise unions chosen in this way; they could not ignore or bust unions as once they had. For the first time in American history, labour was winning substantial support from the federal government. Unions could now take on the major corporations and hope to win. But the shapers of the law also had a wider perspective. Its preamble spoke of the deleterious effects of 'depressing wage rates and the purchasing power of wage earners'. If unions could be strengthened, they would keep up wage rates, and hence there would be more consumer purchasing power in the economy at large. Many businessmen did not understand this, but there were government advisers who were working to this end.

The Wagner Act shifted the focus of labour conflict away from violent confrontation at the picket lines and towards the hearing rooms of the National Labor Relations Board. It also largely shifted jurisdiction in labour disputes from the courts to the NLRB. In regulating labour relations, the act simultaneously constrained labour in a mesh of rules and procedures and powerfully augmented it. Unions might still suffer setbacks, but their institutional security was immeasurably stronger and they could survive reverses more readily. In later years, these strengthened unions were to win impressive wage gains and fringe benefits from employers. The act also incidentally served to enhance the position of men in the labour market, since the great majority of union members were male. Previously, women workers had been accorded some protection in law, as in laws regulating their hours and wages, but men had been seen as free agents, capable of deciding themselves under what terms they would work, and for the most part had been denied protective legislation. Now they could seek protection through their unions. One measure of the effectiveness of the Wagner Act was the considerable decline in the number of workers injured in industrial disputes. The passage of the act greatly aided union recruitment, although it could only become fully effective once the Supreme Court had upheld it in 1937.

The growth in trade union membership was paralleled by a tendency for American workers to shift their allegiance to the Democratic party and to display a greater interest in national politics. In the Republican Midwest in particular, many city workers, locked into a deferential political culture, had in the past voted the same way as their bosses. The class-conscious impulses that led many workers in the 1930s to fight for unions also led them to abandon the Republicans for the Democrats, particularly as the New Deal revealed its pro-labour sympathies. Workers for the first time came to look on government for protection, a major change in their attitude towards the state. These changes in party politics and political expectations cannot be attributed to the Wagner Act, but the act did represent a major step in the mutually supportive accord that was forged between the New Deal and organised labour.

Another epochal measure that implicated the federal government in the marketplace was the Social Security Act of August 1935. The initiative for this came from the administration, as Roosevelt had been pressing for it since January, although only after his renewed call for reform legislation in June did it make it into law. The Depression had wiped out the savings of a great many middle-class and working Americans, and the terror they felt at the prospect of immediate penury and an impoverished old age was reflected in the popularity of the Share-Our-Wealth and Townsend movements. These were among the spurs to Washington policy-makers, but Roosevelt's advisers had long been working on the legislation, and they also saw the economic value of a social security system which would place some purchasing power in the hands of people at large during hard times. On Roosevelt's part, a major motive was to replace the dole. Social security entitlements offered a longer-term alternative to his efforts to offer work relief in place of relief payments, which he saw as 'a narcotic, a subtle destroyer of the human spirit'.

The Social Security Act represents the federal origins of the country's welfare state, whose evolution was to be shaped by the act's principles. The first principle was that of social insurance: workers (and their employers) were to make contributions to establish the workers' rights to old-age pensions. This was to be a national system of old-age pensions (some states had previously made patchy provision). Similarly based on the insurance idea, although administered through a joint federal–state partnership, would be unemployment benefit, since a payroll tax would oblige employers to help fund it. At last a permanent system was being put into place to address the most serious social problem highlighted by the Depression, what to do with the unemployed in an industrial society. The second principle was that of categorical assistance, that is relief to various worthy categories, mainly dependent mothers and children and the physically handicapped. This was again to be a dual system; federal funds were to be supplied to the states in line with state provision. The benefits that came to be paid under the insurance principle were better than those paid under categorical assistance, partly because many states were niggardly in their matching payments. But the differential also resulted from the fateful distinction between contributory social insurance (which seemed to give 'contributors' ownership or an entitlement) and categorical assistance, which was to evolve as rather grudging 'welfare' payments to those who had not made provision for their own support. Thus in the course of time, a category which had once been seen as deserving ('widowed mothers') came to be seen as undeserving ('welfare mothers'). In most other countries, a range of social policies shaded the differences between the various categories of 'deserving' and 'undeserving'; in the United States the distinction was sharpened, albeit somewhat unintentionally.

Nonetheless, even the unemployment compensation levels were modest compared, say, to Britain's, and very large categories (notably domestics, agricultural labourers and the self-employed) were excluded from the pension and unemployment benefit programmes. The Social Security Act also made no provision for health cover, another feature that differentiated it from the welfare states taking shape elsewhere. But whatever its inadequacies, future administrations could and would add to it. As Franklin Roosevelt put it himself, the act was but 'a cornerstone in a structure which is being built but is by no means complete'.

The act was shaped by a volatile mixture of interest group pressures and political calculations. It did little to redistribute income and the employee tax was regressive, but, as Roosevelt said, 'With those taxes in there, no damn politician can ever scrap my social security program.' The act also represented a significant shift in the American approach to welfare. Previously state and local programmes had been largely directed to helping mothers, and women's groups had been prominently involved in them. In this sense the character of early American welfare is sometimes said to be 'maternalist'. The network of professionals and academics who advocated social insurance, on the other hand, were mainly men. Their aim was to avert poverty, and their schemes in effect offered rights mainly to middle-class and upper-working-class males – those with reasonably secure incomes. Unemployment and pension entitlements were to be held by those making contributions from their wage packets. A political virtue of this approach was that it won the support of the middle classes for social security. In affording benefits to men, the New Deal thus deflected American welfare from its original maternalist orientation, although it had created only a 'semi-welfare state'.

Another belated piece of 'must' legislation – as the administration dubbed those measures it considered essential – was the bill which became the Banking Act in August 1935. The objective of this was to make American money and banking somewhat more subject to the will of the president. Despite fierce resistance from private bankers, the act passed and reconstituted the Federal Reserve Board as the Board of Governors of the Federal Reserve System, most members of which would be political appointments, and added to its powers, including the important power to set the rediscount rate or bank rate. Essentially the measure served to enhance the authority of the federal government and to centralise the power of the Federal Reserve System over monetary policy. Finally, and very belatedly in the western world, the United States had a central banking system.

Conservatives had initially seen the banking bill as an attack on private bankers, and other measures of the summer of 1935 also seemed like an assault on business. One was the Public Utility Holding Company Act, a product of the revived interest in the administration in the value of competition. The failings of the NRA had undermined the view that excessive competition had contributed to the depression and given the anti-monopolists among Roosevelt's advisers greater credibility. The nation's electricity was often supplied by enterprises operating at the base of holding company pyramids, and Roosevelt wanted those holding companies that did not seem to be working in the public interest to be broken up. The power companies spent over a million dollars resisting the measure, but while the final act was a little less draconian than the president liked, it did reduce the pyramids and subject the industry to regulation by the Securities and Exchange Commission. It was a blow at sheer bigness in business and it led to the dissolution of several utility structures. Another attack on bigness came with Roosevelt's Wealth Tax Act, or the 'Soak the Successful' tax as the Hearst press called it. Roosevelt had initially proposed a fairly drastic measure, directed in part at corporate and undistributed profits, but again conservative opposition in and out of Congress succeeded in modifying it, this time significantly. Nonetheless the act as passed did increase top personal income tax rates and imposed a progressive income tax on large companies. The redistribution of income was minimal, but the monied interests concluded that they were not loved by the president.

By the autumn of 1935 the great reforming thrust of the New Deal was beginning to weaken. Never again in the Roosevelt years would Congress be subjected to the blitz that it experienced in the second hundred days. Not that Roosevelt himself wished to abandon the cause. During the 1935 reform offensive the New Deal had become more identified with labour and the working classes, and the disenchantment of most of the business community had intensified. The central measures of 1933 had aimed at co-operation between government and commercial, industrial and agricultural business. The measures of 1935 benefited from the advice of a few businessmen and were certainly not anti-capitalist, but generally their framers saw them as strengthening the economy by introducing greater stability, security and fairness. In making the banking system less vulnerable, shoring up unions and putting a little money into the pockets of the needy, who were also consumers, the second hundred days hardly represented a mortal threat to American capitalists. The intention was not to overturn the system but to reallocate some of its benefits, and even then fairly modestly and far from equitably. But for the most part this raft of measures was enacted over the bitter opposition of the major corporate and monied interests.

For the moment the president rested on his laurels, but the presidential campaign of 1936 soon loomed, and class issues continued to figure with unusual prominence. Roosevelt demanded relatively little of the 1936 session of Congress, but some remedial legislation was necessary to contain the ravages of the Supreme Court, and the president did not endear himself to business by another imposition on corporate taxation. The noise from the demagogues like Father Coughlin and Dr Townsend had abated somewhat in the wake of the reform legislation, some improvement in the economy and the death of Huey Long, although Coughlin did try to rally these populist elements behind a newly formed Union party. As usual, however, the election of 1936 was primarily to be a contest between the two major parties, and it could hardly avoid being a kind of referendum on the extraordinary innovations introduced to American life by Franklin Roosevelt in the previous four years.

The Republicans made some modest accommodations to the political climate inaugurated by the New Deal in nominating the moderate Kansas governor Alfred M. Landon for president and in adopting a platform promising assistance to farmers, old-age pensions and the right of labour to bargain collectively. But the platform also denounced the centralising and unconstitutional tendencies of the New Deal and emphasised the Republicans' commitment to reduced federal spending and a balanced budget, to deregulation, and to the role of state and local governments in the areas of relief and social security. The New Deal, it said, had 'dishonored American traditions'. 'America is in peril', it shrieked, threatened by no less than 'Government itself'. Further, the groups that rallied to the Republicans served to draw attention to the party's reactionary wing. Conservative and embittered Democrats like Al Smith and John W. Davies joined with certain big business interests in the Liberty League in denouncing the New Deal and its 'communistic' activities, although by this date the League seemed to be so much the tool of paranoid plutocrats that Alf Landon himself bemoaned its support as the 'kiss of death'. The conservative National Association for Manufacturers also supported the Republican ticket, while unhappy liberal Republicans tended to keep a low profile during the campaign. The vice-presidential candidate, Colonel Frank Knox, brashly insisted that Roosevelt 'has been leading us toward Moscow', and Landon himself eventually began to parrot the right-wing depiction of the New Deal as an 'alien' creation.

The Democrats, of course, renominated Franklin Roosevelt, who in his acceptance speech denounced his new targets, the 'economic royalists'. The Democratic platform ridiculed the Republicans' proposals to return serious economic and social problems to the separate states, and boasted of the administration's success in 'humanising the policies of the Federal Government as they affect the personal, financial, industrial, and agricultural well-being of the American people'. Support for the Democratic ticket was provided by both the new-found Congress of Industrial Organizations, which represented the fast-expanding and class-conscious industrial unions, and the older American Federation of Labor (AFL), the organisation of craft unions which had usually kept aloof from party politics. These great union bodies channelled their assistance through a campaign organisation named Labor's Nonpartisan League, which helped to turn out working people in the Democratic cause. The radical farm elements that had emerged around 1934 also tended to align themselves with the president, as did the American Labor party of New York and the La Follette Progressive party of Wisconsin. Also in the Roosevelt camp were a number of survivors of the progressive movement of the early twentieth century, together with several progressive Republicans.

Never had a major party been so identified with the labour and progressive constituencies, at least since the days of Andrew Jackson and Martin Van Buren in the 1830s, and the Democrats were also counting on carrying the grain belt. If there were still 8 million people without work, there were signs that the economy was picking up and production and employment figures were better than they had been at any time since

1930. Further, millions of Americans had benefited in one way or another from the torrent of New Deal programmes. Roosevelt's personal popularity became apparent when he tried to campaign, for the crowds were so great that they frequently blocked the streets. In his final speech of the campaign he again assailed the 'old enemies', that is 'business and financial monopoly, speculation, reckless banking, class antagonism'. Roosevelt's class rhetoric was unremitting: 'Never before in all our history have these forces been so united against one candidate as they stand today. They are unanimous in their hate for me – and I welcome their hatred.'

The results of the 1936 election confirmed the efficacy of the coalition that had been built to sustain the New Deal since 1932. Roosevelt won a record 60.8 per cent of the popular vote, and carried every state save Maine and Vermont. It was a magnificent personal triumph, and a shot in the arm for democratic processes at a time when totalitarian regimes were consolidating themselves on the European continent, where the event was widely noticed. 'Henceforth democracy has its chief!' rejoiced *Paris-Soir.* 'After his brilliant triumph President Roosevelt has become the statesman on whom every hope is to be pinned if the great liberal and democratic civilization of the west is one day threatened, either by Bolshevism or by autocracy.' Further, the Democrats increased their already large majorities in both houses of Congress. In the Senate a mere 16 Republicans survived to do battle with 76 Democrats. Across the country too, in a multitude of state and local races, the momentum of the popular campaign for Franklin Roosevelt carried Democratic candidates into office. Roosevelt's support to the west of the Mississippi was less marked than in 1932, but the New Deal coalition stood more clearly etched. To the solid South Roosevelt could add the northern cities, supporting him even more emphatically than before, not only because organised labour and the city machines were delivering workers and immigrants but also because African Americans were swinging massively to the Democrats. They, too, the most disadvantaged of Americans, had benefited from the New Deal programmes. The Republican party seemed all but banished. Harold Ickes suggested turning Vermont into a national park to 'protect that rapidly disappearing specimen, the homo Republicanus'.

After his triumphant re-election, Roosevelt renewed the call for reform in his Second Inaugural Address, when he pointed out that 'tens of millions' of American citizens were still denied 'the greater part of what the very lowest standards of today call the necessities of life'. The test of the nation's 'progress', he insisted, was 'whether we provide enough for those who have too little'.

5

Decline of the New Deal

The elections of 1936 had seemed like a magnificent vindication of the New Deal. Americans had given an unprecedented acclamation to the presidency of Franklin Roosevelt, and the large Democratic majorities in Congress could hardly be seen as anything other than an endorsement of his reform programme. Yet in the event the New Deal was not driven forward by the victories of 1936. The remarkable legislative achievements of the summer of 1935 were never to be matched, and while occasional pieces of reform legislation were enacted, by 1938 it was clear that the New Deal was effectively at an end, at least if seen as an attempt to restructure the domestic economic and social order.

In his Second Inaugural Address President Roosevelt issued a new call to arms. He reminded the crowds standing in the pouring rain of all that had been accomplished by the power of government since 1932: 'In fact, in these last four years, we have made the exercise of all power more democratic; for we have begun to bring private autocratic powers into their proper subordination to the public's government.' Here was an image of positive government poised against selfish private interests, government that should be a friend of the weak. Much remained to be done. One third of the nation, he pointed out, was still 'ill-housed, ill-clad, ill-nourished'.

The large Democratic majorities in Congress gave some encouragement to this vision, but they were to prove somewhat misleading. Across the country Democratic candidates in 1936 had been only too pleased to cling to Franklin Roosevelt's ample coat tails, but they did not necessarily share his values. Even before 1936 some congressmen and senators had been suspicious of the direction taken by the New Deal but had muted their opposition in deference to Roosevelt's popularity. While the electorate in 1936 could be said broadly to have endorsed the experiment with big government, the triumph was more for Roosevelt personally than for a clearly articulated ideology. Many of the southern Democrats who contributed to the party's majorities in Congress, for example, were at best lukewarm reformers, conscious that too much change could threaten their command of their communities.

Perhaps they could have been cajoled into accepting another reform package, but in the event Roosevelt stunned the political community in February 1937 with a message that sought not further social legislation but the radical overhaul of the Supreme Court. Up to a point this made sense, since the Court had repeatedly obstructed reform, and Roosevelt could feel that his recent re-election demonstrated a powerful public demand for further New Deal measures. If such reform was to be accomplished, the Supreme Court would have to become more amenable. But in the manner of his offensive Roosevelt had made a major miscalculation. The Supreme Court struggle was at last to make it possible for his critics to mobilise effectively against him.

The Supreme Court, stranded in the conservatism of the 1920s, had shown itself able and willing to cripple the New Deal. In 1935 it had struck down the NRA, and in 1936 it effectively killed off the AAA and destroyed other New Deal measures too. Further, the Court had yet to rule on the major legislation of 1935, and the omens were not good given its penchant for prohibiting government intervention in the economy. Unusually for a president who had served a full term, Roosevelt had been unable to appoint any justices of his own choosing; so, feeling that the election had shown that the Court was defying the popular will, he proposed to remedy matters by asking Congress for an act allowing him to appoint a new justice for every judge over the age of 70. The bill applied to the whole of the federal judiciary, but since six of the nine Supreme Court justices were already over 70, his main target could not be mistaken.

Nonetheless Roosevelt based his case on the efficiency of the judiciary, suggesting that elderly judges could hardly be expected to work at full capacity, an argument that was clearly a flimsy cover for his real objective of placing a liberal majority in the Supreme Court. It was also unlikely to appeal to the several senators who were themselves over 70. Even many of Roosevelt's supporters recoiled at what seemed like a crude attempt to pack the Court. The chair of the House Judiciary Committee summed up one reaction with the remark, 'Boys, here's where I cash in my chips', and the progressive leader Burton K. Wheeler broke with the administration to lead the fight against Court reform in the Senate. Conservatives organised the National Committee to Uphold Constitutional Government to lobby against the proposal and to foster suspicions that Roosevelt was aiming at dictatorship.

As it happened, it was the justices themselves who soon saved the Court. One justice began to side with the liberals while another announced his intention to retire, so that even as the 'Court-packing' bill was still being debated the Court began to uphold New Deal legislation, including the Wagner and Social Security Acts. The need for the bill had thus become less urgent, and it was eventually rejected by the Senate Judiciary Committee. If scarred in the battle, Roosevelt later claimed to have won the war. He was soon able to appoint liberal justices to the Court as the old men retired or died, and he encountered little more resistance from that quarter. No New Deal measure was struck down after 1937. Indeed, in time Roosevelt came to appoint most of the Court's members, and the so-called 'constitutional revolution' was confirmed – the Court had ceased to question the right of the federal authorities to manage the economy, a momentous change in attitude. American government was permitted to join the twentieth century.

But there was a heavy political price to pay. The affair damaged Roosevelt's reputation, with even good friends like Governor Herbert Lehman of New York coming out against the bill. The Democrats were disastrously divided by the measure, those among them who had disliked New Deal reform now having an issue on which they could legitimately oppose the administration. Republicans, western progressives and conservative Democrats were able to make common cause in resisting the plan, and congressional conservatives from both major parties gained valuable experience of bipartisan co-operation. Their success moreover suggested to them that it was after all safe publicly to oppose this most popular of presidents.

The Court fight overlapped with an extraordinary wave of industrial unrest which also harmed the administration politically. The automobile and steel industries had traditionally been dominated by open shop companies; employers had constantly beaten attempts to unionise. But at the end of 1936 and in early 1937 the Union of Automobile Workers forced the mighty General Motors Corporation to shut down, in the highly publicised sit-down strike centring on Flint. The strikers scandalised many by their effrontery in occupying private property. In previous eras troops might have been sent in to break the strike, but in this instance the

New Dealers in both federal and state governments made it clear that this weapon was no longer at the disposal of capital. In February General Motors capitulated and agreed a union contract. A few weeks later, in the steel industry, the giant US Steel also capitulated to union pressure, and these labour victories touched off a great wave of union organisation of unusual intensity. Conservatives throughout the country were appalled both by the challenge to managerial prerogatives and property rights and by the protection afforded the strikers by leading Democratic officials, but the unease over the seizure of factories extended far beyond business interests. It seemed to many that Roosevelt was condoning attacks on property at the same time that he was assaulting the Supreme Court. Did the New Deal have no respect for constitutional rights as traditionally defined?

A sudden plunge in the economy in the summer and fall of 1937 hurt the administration yet further. Earlier in the year it had seemed that something of a recovery had been achieved, although unemployment remained high. But then came the shock. Economic activity plummeted even more sharply than had been the case after the Stock Market Crash of October 1929. In the nine months from August 1937 the Federal Reserve Board's index of industrial production dropped by over a third, and millions of workers were laid off. The 'recession' was precipitated in part by a heavy cutback in government spending, Roosevelt having become worried by the size of the budget deficit. The modest gains that New Deal policies had wrested from the economy were stripped away; unemployment rose from 14.3 to 19.1 per cent. By 1938 there were widespread reports of people starving. In the first five months of that year the relief rolls of Chicago rocketed from 50,000 to 120,000, until the city finally closed its relief stations. In a period of seven months WPA rolls in Detroit soared by 434 per cent. The president, it seemed, had lost his magic touch. Inevitably the administration's critics blamed the 'Roosevelt recession' on the president and on New Deal policies. Roosevelt himself prevaricated, uncertain what to do. Eventually he did agree to a new spending package and by 1939 the economic statistics were once more moving in a favourable direction, but by that time the political damage had been done.

The political difficulties thrown up for the Roosevelt administration by the Court fight, the sit-down strikes and the renewed slump did not altogether arrest reform legislation. The Democrats, after all, still had large majorities in Congress, however unreliable they had become, and when president and congressional liberals acted together they on occasion enjoyed some success.

Franklin Roosevelt had shown little interest in urban housing, and the housing initiatives of the administration had hitherto been modest, despite the establishment of the Federal Housing Administration in 1934, which underwrote private loans to middle-income home-owners or buyers. It was Senator Robert Wagner who championed the cause of public housing, and his bill eventually passed in 1937 when the president was persuaded to throw his weight behind it. The Wagner-Steagall Act established the United States Housing Authority and made funds available for low-cost housing. Little such housing was provided over the next few years, but the act did mark yet another historic 'first' – federal government involvement in public housing. In the future the federal authorities would promote slum clearance and give millions of Americans access to better homes. Poor farmers were not forgotten either. The Farm Tenancy Act of 1937 established the Farm Security Administration, which was to provide loans to farm tenants and sharecroppers so they could acquire their own farms or establish co-operatives, and help to migratory workers, such as medical services and accommodation in purpose-built camps. This act went a little way towards balancing the aid the New Deal had given to better-established farmers.

The fight over the 'Court-packing bill' had given rise to some tentative collusion between conservatives of both parties in Congress, and the sit-down strikes and the recession further aided the formation of a conservative bloc. In December 1937 members of this group issued the Conservative Manifesto, which called for a balanced budget and reduced taxes (especially on business) and which asserted the inviolability of states and property rights. By this date even the vice-president, John Nance Garner of Texas, had soured on the New Deal and was according the conservative bloc the benefit of his prestige. Many of the Democrats elected in 1936, it seemed, particularly those from the South, were not so liberal after all, and the president's missteps encouraged them to resist New Deal measures, in concert with congressional Republicans. They were not wholly successful, but Roosevelt no longer had a compliant Congress, and reform legislation dwindled. One sign of the truculent mood in Congress was the formation in May 1938 of the House Committee on Un-American Activities, which soon focused its suspicious gaze on a number of New Deal agencies.

But in 1938, with the midterm elections still looming and congressmen wary of attacking measures that might be popular with their constituents, reform was still possible. A new AAA law made good some of the damage of the Supreme Court, authorising subsidies for staple products, new marketing quotas, and soil conservation. Another important measure also arising in part from the Supreme Court's action was the Fair

Labor Standards Act, which addressed some of the issues once the preserve of the NRA. The act introduced maximum hours and minimum wages for workers in industries engaged in interstate commerce and strictly regulated the use of child labour. This helped further to reduce sweatshop conditions and the exploitation of children, as it also promptly raised the wages of hundreds of thousands of workers. If industry could not regulate itself, regulation would be imposed on it. A similar attitude was displayed in the administration's continued attempts to combat bigness in business. The president prevailed on Congress to establish the Temporary National Economic Committee, which was empowered to investigate price-fixing and other monopolistic practices, and Thurman Arnold was appointed to the Justice Department to head a new trust-busting drive. It was in 1938, too, that Roosevelt persuaded Congress to combat the recession by resuming large-scale spending on federal projects, so that he now seemed more prepared to embrace Keynesian ideas. He had previously clung to the notion that in principle the budget should be balanced, even if it was not always practicable to do so, which was one reason why his budget deficits were never large enough to lift the country out of depression.

Roosevelt's legislative gains in 1938 were made with difficulty, however, and believing his own popularity to be unimpaired he tried to use it to remove a number of his congressional enemies. During the Democratic primary elections of 1938 Roosevelt endorsed efforts to replace an array of southern and mid-western conservatives with loyal New Dealers. But the attempted 'purge' invited unhappy comparisons with events in Hitler's Germany and Stalin's Soviet Union, and such presidential interference aroused local resentments. Almost all the conservatives were re-elected, and some mid-western liberals lost their seats. The Republicans, too, made a significant comeback in 1938, winning several state governorships and increasing their representation in both houses of Congress. Since some 40 Democrats in the lower house and 20 in the senate had already proved themselves unreliable on administration measures, New Deal liberals could no longer hope to control Congress, despite its formal Democratic majorities. Conservatives had learned that they could publicly confront the president without suffering the wrath of their constituents. Reform legislation now became the exception, and in 1939 Congress was even able to chip away at parts of the New Deal, reducing relief expenditure and terminating a few controversial programmes like the Federal Theatre Project. The greater part of the New Deal edifice remained standing, but if conservatives could not dismantle it, liberals could not add to it. This stand-off was essentially to survive until 1964.

The New Deal coalition itself was being subjected to severe strain. Since 1932, and particularly since 1935, the Democratic party had become increasingly identified with industrial workers, the northern cities, and immigrant and black voters. Rural Democrats were less enamoured of programmes that seemed to help the urban working class than they had been of measures to help agriculture, and many of Roosevelt's congressional critics after 1936 were from rural districts. Some southern Democrats were beginning to perceive in New Deal programmes tendencies that would serve to undermine the traditional economic and racial hierarchies of the South. The minimum wage law cut against the interests of low-wage southern industry, and the various anti-poverty and relief measures gave southern blacks (and poor whites) some alternative to the grudging patronage of white landlords. If most southern blacks were still barred from the polls, some found themselves voting in NLRB-sponsored elections for union representation. There were southern liberals like Florida's Claude Pepper who took heart from such trends, but several leading Democrats who drew their support from racist local elites became fiercely hostile to Franklin Roosevelt and all he stood for. These unreconstructed southerners did not necessarily wholly break with the New Deal electoral coalition, since Democratic party membership remained valuable to them and the southern and northern urban wings of the party needed one another in national elections, but they served as a powerful counterweight to the influence of the liberals.

The weakening of Roosevelt's authority was illustrated by his failure to win congressional approval for reorganisation of the executive branch of government. Roosevelt by temperament was a chaotic administrator, assigning overlapping responsibilities to different people and failing to establish clear lines of command, and the enormous growth of government since 1932 had created something close to administrative anarchy in Washington. The powers of the presidency had increased, but the frugal staffing of the White House had made them difficult to exercise effectively, while the haphazard proliferation of executive agencies meant that the structure of government defied co-ordination and control. Previous presidents had fretted over the managerial failings of the American system of government, but the New Deal greatly compounded them.

The president had been pressing for executive reorganisation since 1937, proposing such remedies as an increase in the staffing of the White House, the creation of new cabinet-level departments and the incorporation of independent agencies within the main government departments. The fight over the 'Court-packing' bill, however, had already provoked accusations of dictatorial intent on Roosevelt's part, and executive reorganisation sparked the same charges from his enemies. Indeed, the measure became known to its critics as the 'dictator bill', a sobriquet which could only be unhelpful at a time when the European dictators were attracting disapproving attention. The bill was lost in 1938, although in 1939 Roosevelt secured a much modified version from Congress. This at least enabled him to issue Executive Order 8248, which established the Executive Office of the President, staffed it with six assistants and brought into it the Bureau of the Budget, taken from the Treasury Department, and the National Resources Planning Board. The president was now a little better equipped to manage the extended machinery of government that the New Deal had created. In future years presidents were to take important new agencies (like the Central Intelligence Agency) under their personal wing in the Executive Office of the President.

Roosevelt's growing difficulties with Congress owed something to signs that his personal popularity was not quite what it had been and that the public was finding New Deal prescriptions less convincing. Between December 1937 and November 1938 Roosevelt's Gallup Poll support slipped from 62.1 to 54 per cent. A poll of June 1938 found that 72 per cent of respondents wanted the administration to be 'more conservative' for the rest of its term, and a poll of March 1939 recorded that 52 per cent thought the administration 'not friendly enough' towards business (as against 9 per cent who thought it 'too friendly'). While organised labour remained strong in its support for the Roosevelt administration, such poll evidence suggested that its recent anti-business image was not an electoral asset. But there was another reason, too, for the weakening of reform sentiment. Another poll had found that the most interesting news story of 1938 was the 'Czech crisis'. By the late 1930s the president, Congress and the public at large were becoming increasingly distracted by threats posed from abroad.

6

Isolationism and foreign dangers

The difficulties encountered by the New Deal during Franklin Roosevelt's second term did not arise exclusively from the domestic scene. Foreign pressures were also obtruding themselves. 'As we plan today for the creation of ever higher standards of living for the people of the United States', said Roosevelt in a radio address in October 1937, 'we are aware that our plans may be most seriously affected by events in the world outside our borders.' Hitherto the New Deal had been predicated on a form of economic nationalism, the assumption that the economic and political destiny of the United States was in her own hands. In 1933 Roosevelt had torpedoed the efforts of the London International Economic Conference to find a solution to the global crisis when he withdrew American participation, deciding that the United States must find her own answer. But after several years of hectic experimentation the economy remained obdurately depressed, suggesting that domestic remedies alone were not enough, while overseas the Great Depression had been undermining the world's political stability.

In 1937 the threats to world peace could hardly be missed. Since 1933 Adolf Hitler had been consolidating Nazism in Germany and had reoccupied the Rhineland, Mussolini's Italy had annexed Ethiopia, and from 1936 these fascist regimes were giving assistance to General Franco in the civil war in Spain. Meanwhile, the military had gained the political ascendancy in Japan and was intensifying Japanese aggression in China. In November 1936 Nazi Germany and Japan signed an Anti-Comintern Pact, which Italy joined in 1937, identifying the Soviet Union as their common foe. It was becoming increasingly difficult for the United States to ignore the rise of fascism or the prospect of a confrontation between fascist and communist totalitarianism. Also, for some the New Deal was a symbol and a test of democracy, the most promising alternative in the economic crisis of the 1930s to the systems personified by Hitler and Stalin.

Roosevelt had never been a committed isolationist, but the economic nationalism of the early New Deal was compatible with the isolationist currents that were then asserting themselves in American public life. These caused him few problems in Latin America, towards which Roosevelt developed his 'good neighbor' policy, forswearing the right claimed by previous presidents to intervene militarily if United States' interests seemed threatened. But isolationism primarily meant isolation from Europe. In 1934–35 a congressional committee chaired by the progressive Republican Gerald P. Nye of North Dakota probed the causes of US participation in the First World War and came to the conclusion that intervention on the side of the Allies in 1917 had been largely at the behest of bankers and munitions exporters who had been profiting from the war. The Nye Committee's findings were powerfully amplified by a flood of popular publications pillorying the 'merchants of death', and the impression grew that young American lives had been lost needlessly in 1917–18. The isolationists argued that the best way to prevent a recurrence was to forbid the export of arms or the extension of loans to any participant in a foreign war, and they secured their objectives in the neutrality acts of 1935–37, measures to which Roosevelt unhappily acceded. While Roosevelt would have preferred legislation which left it to the president's discretion whether to impose an arms embargo against a belligerent nation, Congress allowed little flexibility, and the laws as enacted risked encouraging aggression, for they meant that a victim nation could not look for succour to the United States.

The success of Congress in dictating the terms of foreign policy in the mid-1930s owed something to Roosevelt's preoccupation with domestic issues, but by 1937 he was recognising that the New Deal could not be insulated from the rest of the world. The resumption of Japanese aggression in China, at a time when the fascist powers of Germany and Italy seemed to be consolidating their accord, pointed up the dangers inherent in isolationism. In Chicago in October 1937 Roosevelt challenged isolationist sentiment in his celebrated 'quarantine' speech, suggesting that peace-loving nations 'quarantine' the disease of 'world lawlessness'. An angry isolationist response apparently deterred the administration from proposing specific measures against aggressor nations, although it did begin cautiously to increase defence preparations. Abroad, the international

45

situation continued to deteriorate. In March 1938 Hitler incorporated Austria into the Third Reich, and six months later demanded that Czechoslovakia hand over the German-populated Sudetenland. At Munich Britain and France bought 'peace in our time' by allowing Hitler to dismember Czechoslovakia, but in March 1939 the Nazi dictator seized the whole of that country. Mussolini paralleled Hitler's action by seizing Albania for Italy.

Roosevelt deplored these events but was powerless to influence them. He blamed the neutrality laws for encouraging fascist aggression, but Congress was loath to amend them. In April 1939 Roosevelt called for an international conference to explore ways of keeping the peace, only to have his overtures contemptuously rebuffed by the Axis powers. In August news of the Nazi–Soviet non-aggression pact hit a disbelieving world, an accord which secretly allowed the two participants to carve up part of eastern Europe between them. Confident of the Soviet Union's complicit acquiescence, at the beginning of September Nazi Germany launched its attack on Poland, and Britain and France, which had previously guaranteed Poland's boundaries, were finally obliged to declare war.

Fears of a bloody general war in Europe had been growing among Americans for years, and had been partly responsible for the neutrality legislation. Should war come, they might have their sympathies but they did not want to be embroiled in foreign quarrels, and at the outbreak of the war Roosevelt could only declare US neutrality. 'This nation will remain a neutral nation', he said in a radio talk, 'but I cannot ask that every American remain neutral in thought as well.' In fact, much more than had been the case in the First World War, public opinion identified strongly with the Allied cause, although there was less accord on what the United States should actually do. All could agree that the United States should not enter the war, but while some wanted to ensure this by a rigid application of the neutrality acts, others favoured revising them in a way that would help Britain and France. Towards the end of 1939 Roosevelt finally won from Congress a repeal of the prohibition on the export of arms, although only on condition that American lives would not be put at risk. In purchasing munitions belligerent countries would have to take them away in their own ships – the 'cash and carry' principle. Access to American weapons would give Britain and France some prospect of reducing the arms imbalance between themselves and Nazi Germany, but as with so much neutrality legislation the new law was double-edged. American shipping would now have to keep out of the war zone, freeing Germany to embark on unrestricted submarine warfare.

In December Americans were deeply distressed by the Soviet invasion of Finland, but there was little they could do beyond deplore it. The early months of 1940 witnessed the continuance of the 'phony war', as Hitler bided his time. For the moment US strategy retained some credibility. It was plausible to believe that France's vaunted Maginot Line would hold off the German columns, that Britain would retain naval supremacy, and that the war would settle down to an extended stalemate, eventually perhaps to be won by the Allies if they could be sustained by American supplies. US interests – and the cause of democracy – would be served by a policy of benevolent neutrality.

This complacent vision was shattered by the terrifying events of the spring and summer of 1940. In April Norway and Denmark fell to German guns, in May Holland and Belgium as quickly succumbed, and in June France too capitulated, attacked by Italy from the south as well as by Germany from the north. The collapse of France, which almost no one had foreseen, had momentous consequences. The Allied strategy of containing Germany while sapping her strength through bombing raids and a naval blockade had disastrously failed. Great Britain now stood alone, and during the late summer and autumn Nazi bombs rained down on her cities in preparation for a German invasion. Only the United States could save her.

The bombing of London, graphically described by CBS's Ed Murrow in regular radio broadcasts, sent home to many Americans the sickening lesson already spelled out by the remorseless German sweep across Europe. The United States was vulnerable after all. The president himself pointed out ways in which enemy bombers might reach the United States. And even if an exposed America remained untouched, it could find itself standing alone in a fascist world, bereft of friends and markets. Congress suddenly became much more amenable to voting funds for defence, and in September 1940 it also approved the first peacetime military draft in American history.

The case for protecting Americans by assisting the Allies was becoming ever stronger, although powerful congressional forces remained suspicious of measures that might suck the United States directly into war. In September Roosevelt circumvented Congress by reaching a deal directly with the British Prime Minister Winston Churchill, by which fifty ageing American destroyers were given to Britain in return for the gift of air and naval bases in Bermuda and Newfoundland and long-term leases to several other military bases on British possessions in the Atlantic or Caribbean. Roosevelt presented this as a defensive measure, grandiosely characterising it as 'the most important action in the reinforcement of our national defense…since the Louisiana Purchase'.

Roosevelt's insistence that he was not going to take the country into war was repeated in the presidential election campaign of 1940, when he broke with all precedent by running for a third term. No other New Deal candidate had emerged who commanded widespread support, and the alarming international situation seems to have persuaded Roosevelt to make himself available for a third nomination, which at the national convention was presented as a draft. Popular anxiety over Europe also contributed to the Republicans' decision to choose as their presidential candidate the engaging businessman Wendell Willkie, who like Roosevelt was an internationalist in foreign policy. Both Roosevelt and Willkie favoured helping the Allies while promising that the United States would remain at peace – 'Your boys are not going to be sent into any foreign wars', Roosevelt assured American parents – and Willkie, too, endorsed much of the domestic New Deal. Wendell Willkie fared better against Roosevelt than his previous Republican opponents had done, but the country stuck with the president it knew, Roosevelt again running well in the cities and among the lower income groups.

President Roosevelt may not have intended to send American boys to foreign battlefields, but he was well aware that the Allies desperately needed support if Hitler was not to prevail. It was one thing for the United States to supply weapons, but how could the depleted British treasury pay for them? Roosevelt came up with a new and ingenious solution – 'lend-lease'. The United States would simply lend or lease weapons, food or other supplies to Great Britain (or any other country on which American security depended). Such loaned items would somehow be returned or replaced after the war. This was an extraordinary commitment, a cornucopia of largesse to one side in the European war. As Roosevelt himself described it: 'Suppose my neighbor's home catches fire, and I have a length of garden hose....If he can take my garden hose and connect it up with his hydrant, I may help him to put out his fire.' He would not want paying, just 'my garden hose back after the fire is over'. In fact Congress did attach certain conditions to lend-lease when it passed the bill in March 1941, and goods sometimes had to be paid for. The programme eventually swallowed up some $50 billion, most of it for Britain, although three dozen countries received something.

Lend-lease was presented as a defensive measure, but a greater commitment to the Allied cause short of an outright declaration of war could hardly be imagined. The United States had moved a long way from the proclaimed neutrality of the 1930s. She was now to wage war by proxy, or, as Roosevelt put it, to serve as 'the great arsenal of democracy'. The implementation of the policy took the United States even deeper into the conflict. For lend-lease to succeed, the British ships laden with American goods would need to be protected from German submarines while crossing the North Atlantic. Roosevelt quietly directed American warships into Atlantic waters 'on neutrality patrol', helping British shipping negotiate at least the western half of the Atlantic. Soon the inevitable happened. By the autumn US Navy destroyers were being torpedoed by German U-boats, those 'rattlesnakes of the Atlantic' as Roosevelt called them, and American lives were being lost. For the moment neither the German leader nor the American president was prepared to declare war, although Roosevelt was able to use the incidents to secure the repeal of most of what remained of the neutrality legislation.

But American security was being threatened from more than one direction. Japanese aggression in the Far East had continued. The fall of much of Europe to German might had encouraged Japan's militarists, who had finally won full control of the government in July 1940. Japan, consisting of heavily populated small islands, was dependent on the import of oil and other raw materials, especially from the United States, and her leaders now saw an opportunity to seize the resources it needed closer to home. In September Japanese troops marched into French Indochina, and Roosevelt retaliated by banning the export to Japan of scrap iron and steel. His intention was to deter Japan from further aggression, but the effect was to add to the pressure felt in Japan to seek raw materials elsewhere. Almost simultaneously, the German, Italian and Japanese governments signalled their accord with a Tripartite Pact. For Japan to align herself with these fascist warrior states suggested that the European war could shortly become a world-wide one.

The sudden German invasion of Russia in June 1941 meant that Japan no longer had to worry about a Soviet threat. In July the Japanese government extended its control over the whole of French Indochina, apparently not anticipating that the American president would respond by freezing all Japanese assets in the United States. One (somewhat unintentional) effect of Roosevelt's action was to stop all oil exports to Japan. Both governments realised that they were fast slipping towards war, but frantic diplomatic activity failed to find a solution. The Japanese government concluded that it must seize the oil of the Dutch East Indies, but to do that it needed first to destroy American military power in the Pacific. On 7 December 1941, without warning, Japanese planes struck at the American fleet at Pearl Harbor. On the following day the president appeared before a joint session of Congress, and the two houses declared war on Japan. The Japanese had succeeded in doing something that the president had been unable to accomplish – unite the country in a fierce determination to fight and win the war.

For the United States, war may formally have begun in the Far East, but since the spring of 1941 American naval operations had been assisting the Allies in the North Atlantic. The European war was dramatically transformed in June when Adolf Hitler, unable to invade Britain, suddenly hurled his armies at the Soviet Union. As the Nazi divisions streaked towards Moscow, Winston Churchill urged the American president to give unstinting aid to their potential new partner. If the Red Army could hold off the Germans, Britain might be spared an invasion and Nazi strength might be seriously impaired. Soon millions of dollars' worth of supplies were on their way to the Soviets. An acknowledgement that the United States was already effectively in the war came in August, when Franklin Roosevelt and Winston Churchill met in Newfoundland and drew up the Atlantic Charter, which broadly enunciated the war aims. They renounced territorial aggrandisement for themselves, asserted the right of all peoples to choose their own form of government, and identified as among their goals freedom from fear and want, a fair international economic system, and the disarmament of aggressors. Here was Roosevelt formulating war aims when technically the United States was not at war. Churchill privately recorded that 'The President…said he would wage war, but not declare it.'

Churchill also credited Roosevelt with saying that 'Everything was to be done to force an "incident" that would lead to war.' While Churchill presumably had the war in Europe primarily in mind, it was the destruction of much of the American Pacific fleet at Pearl Harbor that precipitated the United States into war. Three days after the United States had declared war on Japan, Nazi Germany declared war on the United States, and if Roosevelt had been manoeuvring for American military participation in the Second World War, he now had his wish.

Roosevelt had been far from candid with the American people, and his promises during the 1940 campaign that American boys would not be dying in 'foreign' wars had agonised the consciences of some of his aides. But at the time he had probably hoped that full support for the Allies short of war would suffice to contain the fascist threat. 'If Great Britain goes down', he warned his fellow countrymen, 'the Axis powers will control the continents of Europe, Asia, Africa, Australasia, and the high seas – and they will be in a position to bring enormous military and naval resources against this hemisphere.' Everyone in the Americas would be 'living at the point of a gun'. As events in the North Atlantic and the Far East unfolded in 1941 it must have been borne in on Roosevelt that sooner or later the United States would be embroiled in the conflict, and the promulgation of the Atlantic Charter seemed to anticipate this outcome. But, constrained by the isolationists in Congress, he could not take the initiative in declaring war and awaited an enemy attack.

Such circumstances, together with the fact that American intelligence knew that the Japanese were planning an attack, have led some scholars to suggest that Franklin Roosevelt wittingly sacrificed the fleet at Pearl Harbor in order to get the United States into war. The truth is probably less Machiavellian. The Americans did not know exactly where or when the Japanese would strike, and logistically an attack in Southeast Asia and the Philippines seemed more plausible than one on distant Hawaii, where the battleships were allowed to remain in their moorings. American intelligence gathering and its analysis and dissemination were inadequate and slow, but there is no reason to believe that the president connived at the loss of over 2,000 American lives at Pearl Harbor. Rather, as Frances Perkins said of Pearl Harbor, Roosevelt's 'terrible moral problem had been solved by the event'.

'That day ended isolationism for any realist', Senator Arthur Vandenberg was to write of Pearl Harbor. Vandenberg had been a leading isolationist himself, but he was now converted to the internationalist view that American security demanded international co-operation. In fact isolationist sentiment was not dead, but it had been cripplingly weakened, just as from the late 1930s the experiment with strict neutrality had been progressively discredited. Neutrality in the modern world seemed an illusion, isolation a danger. A tradition dating back to George Washington was finally being irrevocably broken. Henceforth American foreign policy would be internationalist in orientation, and for as long as anyone could foresee the United States would be the biggest player on the world stage.

In the summer of 1941 Henry Luce of *Life* magazine had argued that the success of American democracy itself depended on the creation of 'an international moral order', and he looked to all Americans 'to create the first great American century'. Roosevelt, too, had reached the conclusion that the survival of American values was linked to the proper ordering of the wider world, and the Atlantic Charter anticipated the creation of 'a wider and permanent system of general security'. From that point on Roosevelt and other American officials were giving thought to the shape of the post-war world, and their deliberations assumed both that the United States would play a major global role and that there would be an international body charged with attempting to keep the peace.

7

Into the war

By 1941 the United States had retreated a long way from its historic isolationist stance; by the end of the war she was by every reckoning the world's dominant power. The war had done what the New Deal had been unable to do, restore American prosperity, and it left the country immeasurably more powerful than any of her shattered wartime allies or enemies. In the words of the *New York Herald Tribune* in August 1945:

> Every American faces himself and his countrymen with a new confidence, a new sense of power....We cannot if we would shut our eyes to the fact that ours is the supreme position. The Great Republic has come into its own; it stands first among the peoples of the earth.

During his second term in office Franklin Roosevelt had moved away from the political and economic nationalism that he had displayed early in his presidency, and had come to recognise that the security and welfare of the American people could not be guaranteed solely by American decision-makers. It was not simply peace that was at stake but economic security too. The New Deal had sought to restore economic and social wellbeing to the American people, but whatever obstacles it encountered at home it could never really hope to succeed while chaos stalked the world. From the beginning of American involvement in the Second World War, Roosevelt was determined not merely to defeat the Axis powers but also to bring about a healthier international order. It could almost be said that he wanted to extend the New Deal to the rest of the world, to promote human welfare abroad as well as at home. To him, this was a democratic imperative.

Prior to December 1941 the United States was conducting war indirectly, the resources of its vast economy helping to sustain Britain and the Soviet Union against Nazi might and China against the Japanese invaders. When the United States was precipitated directly into war its wealth made it the senior partner. Conduct of the war required close co-operation between the United States and Britain in particular, and on American insistence it was agreed that there should be a unified Anglo-American command, with senior American and British officers forming a Combined Chiefs of Staff in Washington. Ultimate political authority was slipping from London to Washington.

In a sense – and to oversimplify – the Second World War constituted two wars: the European war and the Pacific war. The United States alone played a major role in both, one of the bases for its subsequent claim to global pre-eminence. Geography may have protected the American population, but the American commitment was colossal. During the First World War the American army had only been fully engaged for the last six months; during the Second the United States entered at a low point for the Allies and was to carry the major part of the burden for nearly four years. From 1941 the Second World War became very much an American war, and no one had a greater say in its conduct than Franklin D. Roosevelt.

Roosevelt was determined to play his constitutional role of Comm-ander-in-Chief to the full. 'Dr. New Deal', he told the press, was being replaced by 'Dr. Win-the-War'. The responsibility that rested on him, as the supreme authority in both civil and military spheres, was immense. Under his guidance, public opinion was to be successfully harnessed for the war effort, supportive majorities maintained in Congress, America's vast and complex economy competently mobilised, and huge army and navy forces raised and deployed. At the same time Roosevelt adroitly 'managed' his wartime allies, personified particularly in the formidable figures of Winston Churchill and Joseph Stalin. Roosevelt's style was open to criticism, for he assigned overlapping duties to different aides, delegated tasks to a host of competing agencies, often issued confusing or contradictory instructions, and punctuated his habitual prevarication with seemingly capricious decisions. But this style also served to enhance his authority, for ultimately it was Roosevelt himself who had to strike a balance between the various military, political, economic and other considerations and resolve the conflicting pressures. His Vice-President, Henry Wallace, marvelled at Roosevelt's capacity to 'keep all the balls in the air without losing his own'.

When Japanese planes struck at Pearl Harbor the German army was on the outskirts of Moscow. Meanwhile in the Atlantic German submarines were attacking American shipping. When twenty-six Allied nations incorporated the Atlantic Charter into what they called the United Nations Declaration in January 1942, the prospect of stopping the Axis powers looked remote. For one thing, at this point American mobilisation had not proceeded far and would not be fully accomplished for another year.

Given that the American contribution would initially be limited, an early issue was where its resources should be concentrated. The United States had been attacked in the Pacific, but her allies were primarily fighting the war in Europe and North Africa. The Soviet Union, desperately fending off the Nazi invasion, wanted Britain and the United States to launch an assault across the English Channel and open a second front in France. Roosevelt was open to this idea but Churchill rejected it as premature, remembering the carnage of the First World War; he argued instead that Anglo-American forces should initiate an offensive in North Africa, where the British were already pressing the Germans and Italians and where landings could be effected on Vichy French territory where resistance might be slight. The Axis forces could be caught between an Anglo-American invasion force from the east and a British thrust from Egypt. The American military would have preferred to commit their resources to the Pacific, but Churchill persuaded Roosevelt to undertake a North Africa campaign (see map 1).

The British believed that Hitler's empire might best be undermined by a 'peripheral' strategy, attacking him around the edges, probing for his weak points and obliging him to divide his forces. When German strength was sufficiently depleted, an invasion of the European continent could follow, perhaps launched from North Africa. Roosevelt's decision to back Churchill rather than his own generals illustrates the major role that he played in determining the war strategy. The decision also meant that for the time being the Pacific war would have a lower priority.

General Dwight D. Eisenhower was given overall command of the North African campaign. In October 1942 General Bernard Montgomery's British Eighth Army confronted the forces commanded by General Erwin Rommel at El Alamein and drove them out of Egypt. In the following month Allied troops landed at Oran and Algiers in Algeria and at Casablanca in Morocco. Eisenhower made a deal of a kind with the Vichy French commander, Admiral Jean Darlan, which reduced the possibility of resistance from French troops. Following the Allied invasion of Casablanca and Algeria, Allied troops began pressing east, but the North Africa campaign took longer than anticipated. The Germans and Italians were well entrenched in Tunisia, and American troops experienced some humiliation at Rommel's hands, but in May 1943 the besieged Axis forces finally surrendered to superior fire-power. Some 275,000 German and Italian troops were captured. The Nazis, it seemed, could be beaten after all. Two months later Allied forces, from their bases in North Africa, landed in Sicily. In September they pressed on into Italy, and the Italian government quickly surrendered, although German divisions stopped the Allied advance south of Rome. Nonetheless Allied strategy thus far had been largely successful. The Germans and Italians had been removed from North Africa and Italy had been knocked out of the war.

Meanwhile Roosevelt and Churchill met in secret at Casablanca in January 1943, and the invasion of Sicily and Italy had been planned. This meant delaying the second front in Europe yet again, somewhat to the embarrassment of Roosevelt since he had promised Stalin an invasion of France to take Nazi pressure off the Soviet Union. But the president went a little way towards mollifying the Russians by announcing at a press conference that the Allies would insist on the 'unconditional surrender' of Germany and Japan. There was a risk that this demand would prolong the war, but the message was that Britain and the United States would not desert the Soviet Union, which they hoped would not be tempted to reach its own accord with Hitler as it had in 1939. It was also decided at Casablanca to subject the German military and civilians to continuous pressure through massive bombing raids.

Ironically, the political pressures for opening a second front increased with Soviet victories. In February 1943 Soviet forces won the bloody battle of Leningrad, capturing twenty-two German divisions. Hitler's mighty armies soon fell back under Soviet advances, and by the summer it was being borne in on British and American strategists that the Soviets could reach Berlin first. The Soviet Union might be an ally, but Roosevelt and Churchill had no wish to see German domination of Europe replaced by Russian. There was also the question of where the second front should be launched. The Americans wanted to strike across the English Channel; Churchill still hankered after an invasion of the Continent through the Balkans, but the Americans had established themselves as the dominant partner in the alliance, and a cross-channel operation it would be. To plan it, and to discuss the shape of the post-war world, Roosevelt, Churchill and Stalin met together at Tehran in November 1943, the first meeting of the 'Big Three'.

At Tehran it was agreed that the second front would be opened via an Anglo-American invasion of France early in 1944, Operation Overlord.

But at Tehran, with the end of the war possibly in sight, much more was agreed on. There was to be a United Nations organisation to keep the peace. With the Allied victory, Germany was to be broken up. Even more important, Churchill and Stalin agreed that while some German territory could go to Poland, whose invasion by Hitler had precipitated the European war, the Soviets might take eastern Poland. Mindful of the Polish-American vote back home, Roosevelt could not formally agree, but he quietly acquiesced. The shape of post-war Europe was beginning to glimmer.

Operation Overlord was to be commanded by Dwight Eisenhower. Through the first half of 1944 Allied planes repeatedly bombed German factories, ports and cities, though they encountered fierce German resistance, and it took several months (and the advent of longer-range planes) before they won ascendancy in the skies. Meanwhile massive Allied forces were gathering in England and in June, on D-Day, the greatest amphibious attack in history was launched with the invasion of Normandy. Eventually German resistance was overwhelmed by sheer numbers. The Allied troops crossed France, and towards the end of August Paris was liberated. By that time the Germans had lost some 450,000 men, and the Allies less than 40,000.

But the war in Europe was by no means over. Towards the end of 1944 Hitler determined on a bold counter-offensive, diverting resources from the eastern front and sending 250,000 troops through the Ardennes and towards Antwerp in the hope of piercing the Allies' lines, thus cutting the Allied armies off from one another. This offensive culminated in the Battle of the Bulge of December 1944 and January 1945, which cost the Allies some 60,000 casualties, though German casualties were double that. Meanwhile the Soviets took advantage of the depletion of German forces in the east to launch their own winter offensive, their massive armies quickly smashing across Poland. By February 1945 the Red Army was within 50 miles of Berlin. The Allies pounded at German morale with heightened bombing raids, including the ferocious bombing of Dresden despite its modest military significance. During the spring of 1945 American and British forces pressed into Germany from the west, and at the end of April Soviet troops entered Berlin. At that time Adolf Hitler had committed suicide, and what was left of the German government quickly agreed to unconditional surrender.

But the Americans (and the British) were fighting a war in the Pacific as well as in Europe. After Pearl Harbor Japanese forces quickly pursued their advantage in Southeast Asia and the Pacific. Most of the remaining territories of the European colonial powers quickly succumbed. The

British were turned out of Hong Kong and Borneo, and suffered a massive blow with the capitulation of Singapore, their island stronghold at the tip of the Malay peninsula. Burma, too, succumbed to the Japanese invaders. By April 1942 the Dutch possessions of Sumatra and Java had also fallen to the Japanese. In a matter of months the European empires had been devastated. The Americans suffered humiliations too, as the Japanese seized not only Guam and Wake Island in the Pacific, but also the Philippines. The western Pacific was becoming a Japanese lake, and the Americans' uncertain ally, China, was left even more exposed to Japanese aggression. In the summer of 1942, however, the Americans were able to inflict a crushing naval defeat on the Japanese at the Battle of Midway, frustrating their attempt to win complete ascendancy in the Pacific.

With Japanese expansion in the Pacific arrested, the United States was now able to counterattack (see map 2). American troops landed on Guadalcanal in the Solomon Islands, although the struggle was to prove a long and bloody one, the Japanese eventually abandoning the island in February 1943. The war in the Pacific was finally turning in the Allies' favour. Allied forces could now hope to prevent essential raw materials like oil from reaching the Japanese home islands and to proceed towards Japan and the Asian mainland by seizing groups of islands in the Pacific. The resultant engagements with Japanese forces were often costly in terms of men and weaponry, but the extraordinary resources of the United States prevailed. The greatest naval battle in history was fought at Leyte Gulf in the Philippines in the fall of 1944, crippling the Japanese navy, and in the spring and early summer of 1945 the Americans moved closer to Japan by winning bloody engagements at the islands of Iwo Jima and Okinawa. The heavy casualties that the Japanese were prepared to bear suggested that they would not yield their home islands lightly. None-theless, hoping to burn the Japanese into surrender, the Americans began to direct heavy incendiary bombings against Japanese cities.

But Japan did not surrender, not until the United States released a horrendous new weapon. In August 1945 atomic bombs were dropped on Hiroshima and Nagasaki. Massive firestorms immediately incinerated tens of thousands of people, perhaps some 150,000 in the two cities together. At the same time the Soviet Union declared war on Japan. Some Japanese military leaders wanted to fight on, but Emperor Hirohito decided other-wise. Japan after all surrendered without an invasion, much to the relief of Allied troops around the world. Whatever considerations governed the American decision to use the atomic bomb, an important one was the desire to end the war without further American losses.

By VJ Day the era of Franklin Roosevelt was over. The president had died in April, knowing that Germany was defeated but knowing, too, that further sacrifices would be required in the Pacific. For the bulk of American citizens and for American servicemen around the world, news of Roosevelt's death was stunning. A group of servicemen in the Philippines were too devastated even to observe the conventional rituals of mourning: 'Our feelings were too strong, and he was – there is no getting away from it – the "father of us all" '. Winston Churchill, when given the news, felt that he 'had been struck with a physical blow'. In the same month Benito Mussolini and Adolf Hitler were also to die, and three months later Churchill was swept out of office by the British electorate.

But Franklin Roosevelt had already largely accomplished his objectives. However hesitantly, he had led Americans away from isolationism and all but ensured that the United States would play a commanding role in the new world order. In January 1941 he had told Congress that he wanted a world grounded on the 'four essential freedoms': that is, the freedoms of speech and of religion and freedom from want and from fear. But such ideals (with their echo of American pluralism and New Deal activism) would not preclude a dominant position for the United States. American strategy throughout the war was determined not only by the imperative to win it but also by a determination to fashion a system of international relations on American terms.

Roosevelt's abiding interest in the post-war order had been manifest at each of the conferences he held with Allied leaders. At Casablanca in January 1943 it was made clear that the Nazi empire would be totally destroyed; there would be no place for even a repentant and diminished Hitler in post-war Europe. At Tehran in November it was agreed to establish a United Nations organisation and to dismember Germany, and it was also in effect conceded that eastern Poland would remain under Soviet control. After Tehran Churchill and Roosevelt gave further thought to the fate of Germany; US Secretary of the Treasury Henry Morganthau Jr proposed a plan to keep Germany weak by destroying its industry and making its economy 'primarily agricultural and pastoral in character'. In the event other counsels prevailed as it was realised that a healthy German economy was a prerequisite for a healthy European economy.

Roosevelt, Churchill and Stalin met again at Yalta in February 1945 to discuss the post-war settlement in more detail. They reached accord on the broad shape of the United Nations. Germany was to be divided into four zones, occupied respectively by the United States, the Soviet Union, Great Britain and France. Poland, in Churchill's view, was 'the most important question', but the room for manoeuvre of the western allies was constrained by the brute fact that the Soviet army already occupied that unfortunate country. It was decided to defer agreement on Poland's western frontier, but Britain and the United States reluctantly agreed that Poland's government might be constituted around the Lublin Committee, dominated by Polish–Russian Communists, although some members of the Polish government-in-exile in London were to be included. Stalin promised that a permanent government would be chosen through 'free and unfettered elections as soon as possible'. Given the military and political realities, Roosevelt felt that there was little more he could do to protect Poland. Further, he wanted and secured a Soviet promise to enter the war against Japan, a war which at that point in time was expected to last at least through 1946. Despite the equivocations at Yalta, Roosevelt's decisions there and at the other wartime conferences made him a major architect of the emerging international order.

Roosevelt was intent on the United States playing an active role in the world, though he was not always clear as to the means. At the Atlantic Conference he had at first floated the idea of the United States and Britain together serving as an international police force before deferring to the objective of 'a wider and permanent system of international security'. But Roosevelt had no desire to see another ineffective League of Nations, which he believed had been undermined by too many small countries, and he expected the Allies, the United States chief among them, to have a major voice in the new international institution. He believed that only the strong powers could enforce world peace, and in private he spoke of a post-war order in which 'four policemen' – the US, Britain, the Soviet Union and China – would exercise this role. At Tehran he put it to Stalin that the United Nations might be headed by an executive committee consisting of the Big Four. As the war progressed Roosevelt ceased to press his 'four policemen' idea, but its influence was seen in the final American plan for the United Nations, which accorded a dominant role to a security council of eleven members, of which the Big Four (expanded to Five with the addition of France) would be permanent members.

During the war years the State Department worked hard to bring about the United Nations Organisation, deploying a great propaganda campaign to win over the American people. Resolutions were passed by both houses of Congress in 1943 calling for an international organisation to keep the peace, and a Gallup Poll of May 1944 reported 73 per cent support for the view that the United States 'should take an active part in world affairs after the war'. In his Fourth Inaugural Address in January 1945 Roosevelt concluded: 'We have learned that we cannot live alone, at peace; that our own well-being is dependent on the well-being of other nations far away.' Restoring economic wellbeing had been the objective of the New Deal, and the president in effect was now suggesting that the very success of the New Deal itself would depend on the new international order that was being created. In many respects, in designing the new political and economic institutions by which the world would be governed, the Roosevelt administration could be said to be extending the New Deal to the world.

The structure of the United Nations was planned by the Allies at a conference in August 1944 at Dumbarton Oaks in Washington, DC. It was agreed that there was to be a general assembly in which every country could be represented, and a powerful security council of eleven members, in which the United States, the Soviet Union, Great Britain, France and China would each enjoy a veto power. The post-war world was to be ordered by the Allies. American influence was reflected in the very preamble of the eventual UN Charter, which echoed the American Declaration of Independence by opening with the words 'We the peoples of the United Nations'. Other agencies to emerge from wartime discussions between the Allies included UNESCO, to promote 'international collaboration in the fields of education, science and culture', and the United Nations Relief and Rehabilitation Administration, which poured assistance into countries that the war had reduced to desperate circumstances. Governmental agencies, not private charities, would ease the lot of mankind.

Roosevelt also recognised that the United States would have to act as economic guarantor of the new world order, the economic needs of which were addressed by a conference at Bretton Woods in New Hampshire in July 1944. Officials in the American and British treasuries had been drafting plans for two years, and the Bretton Woods settlement was very much their creation, the United States having the greatest input. Memories of the depression dominated the minds of the delegates. The 1930s had seen not only many peoples of the world ravaged by poverty, but also consequent political tensions which had spawned fascism and war. The Bretton Woods planners were determined these conditions should not recur. Their objective, in the words of one of them, was to 'distribute happiness throughout the earth'.

The key to this goal, it was held, was a global marketplace in which free trade might flourish together with international control over national monetary systems. This would require the creation of international governmental agencies, whose purpose, in the view of Henry Morganthau, was 'to drive the usurious money lenders from the temple of international finance'. Two major institutions were founded. The World Bank was to extend credit to countries to rebuild their economies, and was also to promote the economic development of emerging nations. The International Monetary Fund (IMF) would promote international currency stability, primarily by providing financial assistance to countries with serious balance of payments problems. It was agreed at Bretton Woods that the monetary system would rest on the US dollar and gold. The United States, in effect, would be the world's banker.

The American and British planners at Bretton Woods possessed a New Dealer's faith in government and a suspicion of business, and they looked to governmental or quasi-governmental institutions (like the IMF) to curb the private interests of bankers and businessmen. They also hoped to protect the weak and distressed. In a sense, the IMF tried to place a safety net under national economies much as Roosevelt's social security system placed a net under individuals, while the World Bank could provide assistance for worthy projects much as the WPA had done. Of course, like the domestic New Deal institutions, the new international institutions did not necessarily work as intended and often served to reinforce the advantages of the strong, and like the New Deal too, these new bodies did not fundamentally challenge capitalism. Their objective was to avert the mutually destructive aspects of free enterprise, not replace it.

The Soviet Union eventually declined to ratify the Bretton Woods Agreements, destroying hopes of a truly global system though leaving the West even freer to set the rules. The World Bank and the IMF, which early became largely subject to the will of the American government, also proved no match for the ingenuity of international bankers, and in the event it was the Marshall Plan and other American assistance and military expenditure abroad that made possible the sustained recovery of the European and 'free world' economies. The United Nations, too, failed to fulfil the hopes of its more idealistic planners, and as early as 1947 the Truman Doctrine made it clear that while the United States would continue to play an international role it would do so unilaterally when it so chose. Franklin Roosevelt and his advisers had hoped to create a liberal world order, one shaped by American values though characterised by co-operation between the wartime allies, but in the unsurprising event it was the United States rather than the international institutions themselves that was to call the tune.

8

War and the home front

The Second World War accomplished what the New Deal had not, the rescue of the American economy from the tortures that had been racking it since 1929. Rarely has an economy catapulted from depression to boom as swiftly as did that of the United States during these years. Farmers found hungry markets for their products. Factories hummed through day and night, overtime was plentiful, and workers streamed home to their families with bulging wage packets. Company profits blossomed. Not only did the unemployed disappear into the factories and armed forces, but even groups that New Deal programmes had not specifically targeted, such as African Americans, suddenly found new opportunities. Within three years of Pearl Harbor the American economy was roaring at full throttle, the United States was winning the war, and Franklin Roosevelt had been elected yet again to the presidency.

The war also effected an accommodation of sorts between the Roosevelt administration and the business community. The New Deal assault on big business was largely abandoned as the corporations were recruited to the war effort. Preoccupied by the global conflict, Roosevelt gave little more than rhetorical support to a new reform drive. But the political adjustment was not all in one direction. The Republicans edged closer to the Democrats, their 1944 platform not only following Roosevelt's internationalist lead in foreign policy but also supporting the extension of New Deal programmes like old-age pensions and unemployment benefits. Many businessmen, too, had come to accept that organised labour was a fact of life and that government had a role to play in managing the economy. Class and party conflict did not disappear during the war, but some of the conditions for a post-war political consensus had been created.

In some respects, the American experience of the Second World War was virtually unique. The other major belligerents found their treasuries, their industries and their populations devastated. About as many civilians as men and women in uniform died in the war. But these were traumas that the United States was largely spared. American cities were never bombed and the American mainland never invaded. As John Morton Blum has noted, the great majority of Americans were 'fighting the war on imagination alone'.

The first imperative was mobilisation, both of manpower and of the vast potential of the American economy. The Depression had given Roosevelt some experience of emergency management, and the growth in federal authority during the New Deal meant that he was a little better equipped to conduct a war in 1941 than he would have been in 1933. But the United States was still far from ready. Once in the conflict, Congress extensively delegated its powers to the president, eventually creating something close to a command economy. On paper at least, the president's powers were very far-reaching – powers to conscript men to military service, to allocate essential materials, to direct manpower, to control prices and rents, to ration consumer goods. The New Deal had warily extended the presence of the government in the marketplace; now the sacred principle of free enterprise seemed almost entirely abandoned.

Prior to Pearl Harbor Roosevelt moved slowly, constrained both by isolationist sentiment in Congress and by liberal New Dealers' suspicions of businessmen, whose participation would be essential to any serious mobilisation. New Deal policies had been largely designed to limit production; now the compelling need was to increase it, but the agencies established to effect this were not given adequate authority. Motor companies, for example, at first continued to produce cars for civilian use rather than give priority to defence contracts. Military and commercial customers found themselves competing for raw materials. During 1940 and 1941 contracts were signed for only about a third of the funds that Congress had appropriated for military and lend-lease purposes.

Pearl Harbor concentrated minds, but through much of 1942 several agencies grappled with different aspects of mobilisation. A War Production Board tried to oversee the drive for production. The old Reconstruction Finance Corporation expanded its activities, producing an array of vital goods and services through its subsidiaries. A War Manpower Commission exercised authority over the allocation of labour. An Office of Price

Administration struggled with the difficult task of imposing price controls on consumer goods and eventually with the distinctly unpopular task of rationing them. In October 1942 Roosevelt tried to bring order through the Office of Economic Stabilization, headed by former South Carolina Senator James F. Byrnes, with extensive powers to control wages, prices and profits. 'For all practical purposes', Roosevelt told Byrnes, who was located in the White House, 'you will be assistant President.' Byrnes moved quickly and his power was further enhanced in May 1943 when he was made director of a new super agency, the Office of War Mobilization. Byrnes was adept at expanding his authority and subordinating the needs of the civilian economy to meet military demands. As late as December 1944 he issued his 'work or fight' order, requiring that men in their late thirties excused military service either take jobs in the defence industries or be drafted into military labour battalions. He even succeeded in shutting down the country's racecourses to save petrol, and he courted yet greater unpopularity with an order that all places of public amusement, such as bars and nightclubs, shut at midnight.

Despite the stumbling progress towards mobilisation, impressive results were achieved. In 1939 the United States had spent only $1.3 billion on the military; this rose to $80.5 billion in 1945. Between 1940 and 1945 American industry produced over 100,000 tanks, 300,000 aircraft, some 93,000 ships and over 20 million small arms. The United States was producing some 60 per cent of the Allies' combat munitions by 1944, by which time its war production was about twice that of the three major Axis powers put together. Technically many American weapons (including the Sherman tanks) were inferior to their German counterparts, and it was the sheer quantity of the Allies' armaments that was to win the war. The American economy had the ability to rise to this quantitative challenge. Before Pearl Harbor a Liberty ship could take nearly a year to construct; ultimately, using assembly-line methods, one could be built in a week. But despite the miracles of production, war mobilisation was never directed with the competence that, say, Churchill's small War Cabinet managed in Britain. American industrial mobilisation was not conducted with Prussian efficiency, but nor was that of the Third Reich.

The mobilisation of men also proceeded uncertainly. Preparedness would require a draft, but even as France was falling to Nazi tanks in June 1940 Roosevelt was reluctant to call for one. There was simply no precedent for a peacetime draft and well-placed isolationists were against it. Not until August, after opinion polls had shown support, did the president endorse selective service, which was enacted in September. Expanding the armed forces meant building new army camps, greatly extending training facilities, and supplying the recruits with equipment and uniforms, all major logistical feats given the extraordinary explosion in military personnel. For most of the 1930s the number on active duty in the armed forces had usually been about a quarter of a million; by July 1941 the figure had ballooned to 1.8 million and in 1945 it reached over 12 million. Altogether a hefty 12 per cent of the population was to wear uniform.

Putting the country on a war footing also meant improving its internal security, for which Roosevelt was prepared to tolerate some erosion of civil liberties. He allowed J. Edgar Hoover's FBI to expand its surveillance activities. The most serious abuse of civil liberties was suffered by Japanese Americans, living mainly on the West Coast. Some of these were Japanese-born and technically still aliens, but 80,000 were *nisei*, or American citizens born in the United States. Japanese Americans had long been the victims of prejudice, but they were ill prepared for the vengeful behaviour that overtook them after Pearl Harbor. An emotional distrust of this Asian presence coursed through many white Americans, western state officials and bureaucrats in Washington, particularly after an American ship was torpedoed off the California coast by a Japanese submarine in December 1941 and as Japanese forces swept across the western Pacific early in 1942. West Coast residents felt vulnerable. In February Roosevelt authorised the relocation of Japanese Americans in the interests of national security, and by the summer most had been interned. Some 112,000 people of Japanese descent, most of them American citizens, had to abandon their homes, jobs and possessions and suffer confinement in overcrowded camps, and the Supreme Court upheld their detention as a necessary war measure. The policy became more difficult to justify as the Americans began to win the Pacific war and it was abandoned at the end of 1944. There was no evidence of subversive intent among Japanese Americans, and some of them in fact were released from the camps to serve in the war, one *nisei* combat unit emerging as the most decorated in the entire United States army.

The mass of Americans were more directly affected by another wartime imperative, the need to pay for mobilisation. The emergency made possible an ingenious restructuring of the national taxation system. Roosevelt's earlier attempt to impose heavier taxes on the rich had been largely frustrated, but he did find a way of tapping the bulging wage packets of wartime workers. Before the war only a small proportion of American adults paid federal income tax, less than 4 million in 1939. The Revenue Act of 1942 lowered personal allowances, bringing many more into the system, and by 1945 nearly 43 million Americans paid federal income tax. Tax collecting also became more secure with the introduction of 'pay-as-you-earn'. The new tax structure was broadly accepted as tolerably just, despite its sweeping extension to lower income earners. Government revenues were enormously increased. In 1940 total federal government revenue was just $7 billion; by 1944 it was over $51 billion. The amount generated by personal income tax alone had increased twenty times. New Deal benefits had given many ordinary citizens for the first time a direct interest in the activities of the federal government; now they had another interest.

Nevertheless, the greater part of the war cost had to be funded by borrowing. During the depression the national debt had grown, to reach an unprecedented 43 per cent of GNP in June 1940, but it exploded to a phenomenal 129 per cent by June 1946. The public provided some of this by subscribing to war bonds, but increasingly important was the role of the Federal Reserve System, which administered these huge sums and whose member banks bought up much of the debt, as did private banks and other financial institutions. In short, the banking system that the New Deal had restructured largely managed these complex operations in deficit financing.

During the war such deficit spending achieved new respectability. The budget deficits that conservatives had deplored in the 1930s had reached $4.4 billion at their most extravagant in 1936, but this seemed risibly timid when compared to wartime spending, the deficit reaching $54 billion in 1943. Dr. Win-the-War was far more profligate with public money than Dr. New Deal had ever been, but won more support. The GNP responded in the vigorous way predicted by Keynesian economics. It had been $85.2 billion in 1938 but in 1940 topped $100 billion for the first time since 1929 and then took off in an extraordinary way, reaching $213.6 billion in 1945. Even allowing for inflation, GNP increased by 70 per cent between 1939 and 1945. The war had done much to vindicate government involvement in the economy.

This ebullient growth meant that unemployment all but disappeared. During the 'Roosevelt recession' of 1937–38 unemployment had risen again to over 10 million, but by 1941 it was down dramatically, to 5.6 million, and by 1944 to a mere 670,000, a tiny 1.2 per cent of the civilian workforce. As the war ended the number without jobs crept up again, but only to 3 or 4 per cent, not to the terrifying figures of the depression. Massive deficit spending had vanquished the scourge of the 1930s. Even some businessmen were converted to Keynesian economics by this extraordinary experience.

American farmers, whose plight had so worried Franklin Roosevelt and his New Deal advisers, were finally delivered from years of trauma.

While some foreign markets collapsed, domestic demand increased and the war precipitated a restructuring of the agricultural economy. In a brief five years a fifth of the farm population swarmed off the land for the opportunities afforded by the cities or the military. For those that remained, the increased use of fertilisers and farm machinery helped to increase productivity. Farm income had long lagged pitifully behind non-farm income, but during the war the gap between the two narrowed. The per capita personal income of farmers more than doubled between 1940 and 1945. Government intervention eased the process of change, as Congress generously increased price supports to farm produce to encourage production. The hardships of the farmer had preceded the depression, and the New Deal had been able to deliver only limited relief, but the war virtually revolutionised agriculture and held out the possibility of prolonged good times. Farmers looked to government to sustain them.

The war also had a major impact on the structure of industry. Corporate profits, even after substantial tax bites, mushroomed from a total value of $6 billion in 1939 to $10.5 billion in 1945. Vast sums of money had been gushing into the corporate sector, or at least into parts of it. Since 1933 the number of individual businesses had been slowly increasing, but from 1941 this trend was suddenly reversed. During the war small businesses were in danger of disappearing. In 1940 there were nearly 3.3 million firms; in 1943 only 2.9 million. Defence contracts usually went to the bigger corporations, partly because they had the capacity to fill large orders. The war allowed big businesses to achieve a massive penetration of the market. In 1940 some 70 per cent of manufactured goods was produced by 175,000 firms; by March 1943 just 100 corporations were supplying that proportion.

As in the early critical days of the New Deal, Roosevelt was again seeking to work with big business. War legislation gave him extensive powers to direct the economy, but it was felt that industrial co-operation would be more readily secured by persuasion than coercion. As Secretary of War Henry L. Stimson explained: 'If you are going to try to go to war, or to prepare for war in a capitalist country, you have got to let business make money out of the process or business won't work.' In 1942 Roosevelt largely abandoned anti-trust action. Businessmen were recruited in large numbers to the mobilisation agencies. Many executives remained on their company payrolls, but served government as 'dollar-a-year men', infusing the public agencies they managed with business values. Tax write-offs were used to encourage firms to switch to war production, and public subsidies were made available to expand capacity. The hostility that had existed between the administration and much of the business community in the late 1930s was replaced by an ambiguous intimacy. The closerelationships between government, business and the military in these years helped to forge what became known as 'the military-industrial complex'.

The rewards accorded to big business were politically palatable because many ordinary Americans prospered too. The war both boosted wage rates and afforded more opportunities for overtime, so that for working people take-home pay increased substantially. In the 1930s, for production workers in manufacturing industries, average weekly earnings had fluctuated either side of $20. In 1944 they reached over $46. Not only did earnings double, but many homes enjoyed the experience of two wage-earners for the first time. Despite wartime shortages, Americans found goods and services to buy. The amount spent by the average urban family on food and beverages jumped from $706 in 1941 to $947 in 1944. But the war distorted consumption patterns, restrictions meaning that less was spent on such items as motorcars and recreation. Instead people hoarded their money. Total personal savings in the national economy during the depression years had been meagre, peaking at $3.74 billion in 1937; in 1944 they reached the incredible total of nearly $37 billion. This figure fell off dramatically in the post-war period as Americans were finally able to spend their enforced savings.

As people surged into the workforce, they also enhanced their security by joining trade unions. Needing the co-operation of unions during the war, the government continued to offer what aid it could to labour. Defence contracts, for example, were used to encourage conservative companies like Ford to concede union recognition. Union membership jumped from 8.9 million in 1940 to 14.8 million in 1945, an historic high at nearly 36 per cent of the non-agricultural workforce. But, in the interests of war production, CIO and AFL leaders agreed to a no-strike pledge and the number of major stoppages declined in 1942 and 1943, although labour's patriotic image was not helped by a spurt of wildcat strikes. The War Labor Board tended to push for more formal grievance procedures, so that disputes would be resolved through bureaucratic rather than industrial action. The war, with its consequent return of full employment and a government anxious to maintain production, enabled the industrial unions to grow and to root themselves yet more firmly in America's political economy, even as it further enmeshed their members in the labour and governmental bureaucracy that the New Deal had spawned.

The jobs explosion, and the diversion of many young men into the armed forces, not only sucked up the unemployed but also pulled in many new workers. More disabled and elderly Americans found that employers now welcomed their services. School attendance of children over 14 actually declined between 1940 and 1944 as some of them found jobs; the number of 14-to-17-year olds who were employed more than doubled. When women joined the workforce the media celebrated the role of 'Rosie the Riveter', overlooking the fact that boys in their mid-teens were becoming riveters too, just as they were also put to work on farms and in offices.

Of more profound significance were the broadened economic opportunities for African Americans. The exigencies of war served to sharpen black aspirations. Racial discrimination did not disappear, but the insatiable demand for manpower eroded some of the old barriers. Blacks appeared on shopfloors that hitherto had been the preserve of whites. The number of African Americans employed in industry, public utilities and transportation doubled between 1940 and 1944. And they were visibly being recruited to the war effort. In 1941 the leading black trade unionist, A. Philip Randolph, threatened a great march on Washington to protest against job discrimination but called it off when Roosevelt issued Executive Order 8802, banning discrimination in federal employment and the defence industries and establishing the Fair Employment Practices Commission to champion minority rights in the labour market. Prodded by government and civil rights groups, the defence industries raised the black share of jobs from 3 per cent in 1942 to 8.6 per cent in 1945, edging closer to African Americans' 9.8 per cent share of the population. The quality of jobs was also tending to improve, as more blacks secured skilled jobs or became foremen.

Franklin Roosevelt could claim a little credit for easing the passage of blacks out of their traditional stations. Government provided something of an example, with the war years witnessing a trebling of African Americans in federal employment. The administration was also sensitive to the black demand to fight. The armed services were prevailed on to recruit more blacks, which they did with some reluctance, often assigning them to support rather than combat roles. Still, the war gave over a million African Americans an experience of military service. The services remained largely segregated, but sometimes logistics forced integration; some African Americans did find their way to the front, and in any case the war introduced them to new skills and to service overseas. Their patriotism attested by military service, black veterans tended to return with enhanced expectations. 'After the close of hostilities', said one black soldier, 'we just kept on fighting. It's just that simple.'

The pressures of war also relocated many blacks. The great exodus of blacks from the southern countryside swelled, as they moved to the cities and to the North, where they found jobs and voted for Roosevelt's party. Relocation came with a price, the resentment of urban residents protective of their own neighbourhoods jobs and schools. Detroit, the heart of the defence industry, experienced rapid growth as southern whites and blacks poured in, and racial tension too. In 1943 a vicious race riot there resulted in the deaths of 25 blacks and 9 whites, and racial disturbances also occurred elsewhere. Suffering from racial abuse, too, were Mexican Americans, similarly drawn by the war demand for labour in the Southwest and California, and some of them were victims of the 'zoot suit riots' in Los Angeles in 1943, so-called because of the clothing then fashionable among young black and Latin males.

The war also changed the lives of many American women, whose employment increased at an even faster rate than that of men. It was primarily married women who met the labour demand. Between the two world wars the proportion of women at work had remained stuck at about a quarter; by 1945 it had jumped to nearly 36 per cent. The war particularly accelerated the trend for married and older women to join the workforce, doubling the number of employed wives. In fact, the need to care for families prompted relatively high absenteeism among them, encouraging Congress to pass the Lanham Act in 1943, providing modest funding for child-care facilities. Government and media encouraged this wartime mobilisation of women. They lauded the 'Janes Who Make the Planes'. Women went into the shipyards and the aircraft factories, training as fitters and electricians. In aircraft engine plants the proportion of employees who were women reached 31 per cent, and in certain delicate tasks, such as wiring junction boxes, they were found to be faster than men. Some women replaced men as bank clerks and cab drivers, and many joined the fast-expanding bureaucracy that the war generated – a million were given clerical jobs in government. If some women lost their jobs after 1945, many held on to them or found others.

The economic growth and the new employment patterns were accompanied by some lessening in class differentials, at least as measured by family incomes. Broadly, most families prospered in these boom years, but the poorest increased their incomes at a faster rate than the rich. Between 1941 and 1945 the lowest fifth of families increased their incomes by 111.5 per cent, while the highest fifth managed an increase of only 55.7 per cent. The resulting redistribution of income in fact was not very great (though it should be noted that the New Deal had not succeeded in redistributing income in the 1930s), and the narrowing of the gap was not continued into the post-war decades. Nevertheless, however modestly, the war had brought greater income equality, in contrast to the economic processes of much of the twentieth century.

The relative good times experienced by many Americans may account for the difficulty experienced by liberals in rekindling interest in reform. Franklin Roosevelt and his advisers had not abandoned their New Deal aspirations, although they were revising them, displaying somewhat less interest in contesting capitalist structures and more in promoting social justice through spending and welfare policies. In 1943 the National Resources Planning Board called for dramatic expansions of welfare, including medical care, and in 1944 Roosevelt proposed an Economic Bill of Rights, attacked business monopoly and made full employment a goal. But, apart from the generous benefits poured on veterans by the GI Bill of 1944, Congress and the public at large were largely unmoved by these calls. Democratic majorities in Congress had been sharply reduced by the midterm elections of 1942 and while the 1944 elections allowed them to regain some ground in the lower house, the same was not true of the senate. A conservative Congress eroded some of the surviving New Deal programmes. Asked in a Gallup Poll of August 1943 whether after the war they would like to see 'many changes or reforms…or have the country remain pretty much the way it was before the war', some 58 per cent of respondents wanted no reforms, and of the 32 per cent interested in change about half wanted to undo the New Deal. Another poll in 1945 found that over half wanted the country to 'stay the same'.

This conservative mood was reflected in public attitudes towards business and labour. Businessmen enjoyed a rehabilitation. The depression had robbed business leaders of their status as public heroes, but war rescued them. The administration itself, of course, wooed the business community, many of whose members were recruited to head government agencies, and business churned out munitions in awesome quantities. Although businessmen were being disingenuous when they claimed to have won the war (overlooking the role of government spending and direction), they won much of the credit. The same could not be said for organised labour. Unprecedented numbers of workers may have been joining unions, but wartime strikes were widely condemned. In July 1945 an opinion poll found that 60 per cent wanted to change the law in ways that would disadvantage labour; only 4 per cent wanted changes favouring unions.

Christopher Thorne has remarked of the Second World War that where 'most of the societies involved, to put it crudely, turned "leftwards" in consequence, American society turned further to the right'. It might equally be said that the war served to expand the centre. The New Deal had always been more about saving capitalism than eroding it, though it contained some who dreamed of using government to redistribute power and exercise economic control. But by the 1940s interest in radical restructuring was fading. The conservative coalition in Congress remained a block on liberal reform, and the recovery of confidence in business tended to marginalise the radicals. Business manipulation of wartime controls had undermined liberal confidence in regulation, while the war revived faith in the capacity of capitalism for growth. By 1945 liberals, probably including FDR himself, were less interested in directly controlling the economy and more in Keynesian-style management and in growth.

But a similar argument could be made for American conservatives. Republicans and businessmen had come to accept many New Deal achievements, like social security and collective bargaining, and the war helped to reconcile many of them to the greater role of government, as it also challenged the Republican party to embrace an internationalist foreign policy. Future prosperity would depend in part on a continuing, if limited, partnership between big business and government in managing a consumer-oriented economy. Many of government's emergency powers would be abandoned in the post-war period, but its authority had been permanently enhanced, as illustrated by the enlarged size of the civil service, and its use of fiscal policy and its new world role could serve business ends. In the post-war years a degree of consensus on broad political and economic strategies would emerge between the major parties.

Conclusion

Franklin D. Roosevelt owed his initial election as president and his later re-elections to crisis, first that of the Great Depression and later that of world war. These crises, together with the responses offered to them by Roosevelt's prolonged administration, were to transform American life. In a land dedicated to the pursuit of happiness, individual Americans came to enjoy a measure of protection from the arbitrary strokes of fate. An economy founded on the principles of free enterprise was fitted with stabilising mechanisms and its major centres of economic power were rendered more accountable. A vast and sometimes decaying landscape was covered with highways, buildings, forests and parks, and a great rural hinterland was lit up with electricity. A governmental structure originally fashioned in and for the eighteenth century was overhauled to meet the needs of a highly urbanised and industrialised society. A nation that had taken pride in standing aloof from the Old World assumed the mantle of global leadership.

Roosevelt's legacy has not been admired by all Americans, but few have doubted his stature. Scholarly studies of the president have always included both favourable and unfavourable assessments, and often biographical treatments have been coloured by the authors' views of the New Deal and of the president's handling of foreign affairs. Political scientists have been drawn to study Roosevelt as 'the first modern president'. For the most part, liberal scholars of the 1950s and 1960s offered sympathetic (if not uncritical) analyses of Roosevelt's stewardship; one of the most influential biographers, James MacGregor Burns, regretted that Roosevelt had not done more to restructure the Democratic party along liberal lines. By the end of the 1960s New Left scholars were advancing critiques reproving Roosevelt for his conservatism and class-based elitism, while the growth of intellectual conservatism in the 1970s and 1980s meant that he was conversely faulted for encouraging the rise of big government. But these jabs from both left and right have done little to dent Franklin Roosevelt's reputation. In a poll of American historians conducted in 1983 Roosevelt was rated as the second greatest US president, denied first place only by Abraham Lincoln. Recent revelations about Roosevelt's private life have reinvigorated the biographical approach, and sympathetic scholars like Doris Kearns Goodwin have examined the complex relationship between Franklin and his redoubtable wife, Eleanor, exploring the degree to which the Roosevelt presidency was a partnership.

'Government has a final responsibility for the well-being of its citizenship', observed Franklin Roosevelt in 1938, and it was this conception that was to be the lasting testament of the New Deal. However imperfectly, Franklin Roosevelt equipped the government with instruments for managing the economy and for conducting social policy. State and city governments, too, were encouraged to assume more responsibility, and when Roosevelt turned his attention to a wider stage he promoted the creation of new international agencies that would have at least some governing functions. A better regulated world, he believed, would serve the well-being of Americans in particular and humankind in general.

This view did not betray a lack of confidence in capitalism so much as a faith in the benign potential of government. Roosevelt had no intention of undermining private property, but he did believe that government action could ease economic distress, curb abuses and render capitalism a little more humane. Previously, the federal government, in so far as it had exercised its authority, had done so primarily on behalf of business. Under the New Deal government was never an obedient client of big business, and while businessmen and financiers could still gain access to it, so could other economic and social interests. The New Deal developed the 'broker state', with government serving as a reasonably disinterested referee between competing lobbies. American government came more fully to reflect the diversity of the American social order, responding to the demands, say, of farmers, urban workers, the elderly and African Americans, as well as of Anglo-Saxon business elites. Women, Catholics, Jews and African Americans were recruited to the federal bureaucracy in unprecedented numbers.

However the Roosevelt administration was more than a simple arbiter between the competitors in a pluralist society. It recruited large numbers of experts to the bureaucracy and regularly advanced its own solutions, even on occasion generating interests which were to become pressure groups in their own right. The AAA programme, for example, led to the creation of growers' organisations that in turn were able to influence agricultural policies. The Wagner Act was more the creation of liberals in the administration and Congress than of the labour movement itself, but it served greatly to strengthen organised labour as an institution. Other measures, such as the Social Security Act and the Banking Act of 1935, could also be seen as more the work of bureaucrats and experts implementing a vision of government than the end result of the interplay of private lobbies, however many concessions had to be made to congressional interests. Specialists, perhaps professors recruited from the universities, became familiar figures in American government, subtly changing its nature. Many of the agencies established in these years, such as the Securities and Exchange Commission, enjoyed the authority to set their own rules, subjecting a wide range of activities to regulations that the president himself would not have anticipated. During the Roosevelt administration the state became a political force in its own right. Roosevelt, it could be said, made politics important. An attempt to deploy governmental-style regulations and institutions to counter private interests across national boundaries similarly underlay the Bretton Woods accords, which were regarded with deep suspicion by Wall Street.

In attempting to introduce a little civility to the capitalist jungle, the New Deal – and the subsequent measures of the war years – profoundly altered the character of American industrial relations. In throwing its weight behind organised labour, the Roosevelt administration effected a more equitable balance between capital and labour. It also drew corporate leaders and trade unionists into an ordered bargaining system, directing them along routes intended to reduce industrial disruption. In legitimising and strengthening the trade unions, the Roosevelt measures helped them to secure for their members the generous wages and fringe benefits that they were to enjoy for at least a generation after the Second World War.

The New Deal's labour reforms have sometimes been seen as an attempt to co-opt labour to the capitalist enterprise, by creating more stable conditions and averting the spread of radicalism. Indeed, some scholars have argued that the New Deal as a whole served the ends of corporate capitalism. In this view, the New Deal was essentially conservative and elite-dominated, and as such it failed to redistribute income, left corporate concentrations intact or even strengthened, ignored issues of race, and was more likely to aid the strong (like large farmers) than the weak (like sharecroppers). All this is fair comment. That it failed to redistribute political power is arguable. It might be fairer to suggest that Roosevelt thought capitalism too important to be left to the capitalists. In a sense New Deal reform did serve American capitalism by giving it an acceptable face, but almost all its major measures, including the Wagner Act, were introduced against the will of the bulk of American businessmen and financiers.

In expanding the authority of government Roosevelt was also enhancing the authority of the presidential office, a process further accelerated by the degree to which he was able to replace an isolationist with an internationalist foreign policy. While presidents continued to be frustrated by the division of powers in the American system of government, henceforth the initiative was assumed to lie with the White House. A president was expected to submit a detailed legislative programme to Congress in a way that had not previously obtained; he was to be the principal policy-maker. Roosevelt's creation of the Executive Office of the President went some way towards ensuring that the president could perform this heightened leadership role, and his successful manipulation of the media to project his personality and further his policy objectives pointed in the direction of the television campaigns and the soundbites of his successors. This new activism of the executive, however, was to bring it into frequent conflict with Congress, that repository of localist interests. Even during Roosevelt's presidency Congress frequently revised the administration's bills in ways the president disliked, and friction between the executive and legislative branches of government would continue to be a major characteristic of American politics. Roosevelt's dominance and political longevity provoked the adoption of the 22nd Amendment to the Constitution in 1951, confining a president to two terms.

Roosevelt's New Deal, and the measures of the war years, not only reached into almost every facet of American economic and social life but also bequeathed institutions, practices and relationships that were to survive for decades. To these years can be traced many of the features which define the modern United States, although some were unforeseen consequences of the administration's initiatives. The New Deal gave birth to the American 'semi-welfare state', which greatly extended social rights even as it deepened the distinction between the 'deserving' and the 'undeserving'. Roosevelt would have been unhappy about the burgeoning welfare roles of later years. His administration also fashioned the distinctive system of industrial relations that continues to be supervised by the NLRB. New Deal and wartime policies did something to reduce the disparity in incomes between farmers and others, and price-support loans continued to sustain American farms, although as a gentleman farmer

Roosevelt had never intended to bring about the massive decline in farm population. Americans know that their mortgages and bank savings are safe because of federal guarantees introduced under Roosevelt. The controls on the stock market and the share operations of business corporations have been the envy of other countries, and, despite the deregulation of the Reagan years, a host of regulations originating in the 1930s continues to restrain the behaviour of American business.

Roosevelt's stewardship endowed the United States with a central banking system, not to mention an expanded federal income tax that still ensnares most working adults. Physical legacies of the New Deal are to be found in a legion of roads and buildings scattered over the land, and in the TVA dams that still provide electricity, while the very modesty of the stock of public housing also owes something to Roosevelt's priorities. From the Roosevelt years, too, emerged a strengthened FBI and an enlarged military establishment: some would say a disturbingly powerful national security state. The city of Washington finally became the American capital in reality as well as in name. In the aftermath of Roosevelt's encounter with the Supreme Court, too, the Court abandoned its 'hands-off' attitude towards governmental intrusions in economic and social matters, and the liberal justices he appointed promoted the Court's growing interest in citizenship entitlements and civil rights. And also operating primarily from American soil are other institutions that owe something to Roosevelt, notably the UN, the IMF and the World Bank.

Surviving for a generation, too, was the political order fashioned by Franklin Roosevelt. The New Deal itself, as a series of economic and social reform measures, lasted only from 1933 to 1938. But the larger New Deal system of politics lasted at least until the late 1960s. Through those years the Democratic party was the majority party, and it broadly identified itself with a liberal agenda, if liberalism is defined in its modern sense as a faith in the benign capacity of government, an acceptance of a mixed economy, sympathy for a modest welfare state, and some sensitivity to labour and ethnic constituencies. During these decades most if not all Republican leaders also bowed to the New Deal agenda in accepting the structures that Roosevelt had created. This is not to suggest that Congress was kept busy with reform legislation, for the conservative bloc in that body was generally able to frustrate or modify the proposals emanating from the White House. But the potential for reform remained. When President John F. Kennedy was assassinated and public opinion rallied behind his programme, and when Lyndon Johnson's election to the presidency in 1964 was accompanied by landslide victories in Congress, the conservative bloc was overwhelmed. The mid-1960s witnessed a whirlwind of reform legislation comparable to that of the mid-1930s. President Johnson himself, a warm supporter of Roosevelt as a young man, saw his Great Society reforms as a kind of revival and completion of the New Deal. 'He was like a daddy to me', said Johnson of Franklin D. Roosevelt.

The ascendancy of the Democratic party in the middle third of the twentieth century arose not only from the voter realignments of the 1930s, as urban working and middle classes and African Americans lined up more firmly behind that party. It rested also on the longevity of the New Deal coalition. The alignment of voting groups that had taken shape in the 1930s broadly survived for thirty or so years. The Solid South, big city machines, the industrial unions, urban white ethnics and African Americans uneasily cohered to give the Democratic party its majorities. It also gave the Democratic party its split personality, for its southern wing became increasingly conservative as its northern elements proved sympathetic to civil rights. Ultimately the coalition eroded, as southern white racists and urban ethnics recoiled at aspects of Lyndon Johnson's Great Society. But it had dominated American politics for more than a generation.

Enduring also was the relationship established under Franklin Roosevelt between the United States and the rest of the world. If the remainder of the twentieth century was not to live up to Henry Luce's vision of the 'American Century', the appellation has at least some credibility. 'When FDR died in 1945, America was more supreme than Great Britain after Waterloo, than the France of Louis XIV, than any power since the Roman Empire', George Will has written. In Germany, Italy and Japan, the wartime allies, particularly the United States, saw to it that new regimes were created which were compatible with American political and economic philosophy. The IMF and the World Bank to a large degree became the instruments of American policy, and the successes and failures of the United Nations have been closely related to the attitudes towards it of the United States. Winston Churchill's epitaph on Franklin Roosevelt was as apt as any when he said that the president had 'altered decisively and permanently, the social axis, the moral axis, of mankind by involving the New World inexorably and irrevocably in the fortunes of the old'.

Select bibliography

Introductory works

There are relatively few books that encompass both the New Deal and the war years, though of course they will be covered in texts on twentieth-century American history. Among the latter is William A. Link and Arthur S. Link, *The Twentieth Century: A Brief History in Two Volumes* (Arlington Heights IL: Harlan Davidson, 2nd edn, 1992), and, from a more radical perspective, Gabriel Kolko, *Main Currents in Modern American History* (New York: Harper & Row, 1976). The whole of FDR's presidency is succinctly treated in Dexter Perkins, *The New Age of Franklin Roosevelt, 1932–45* (Chicago: University of Chicago Press, 1957), and Hoover's as well in Richard S. Kirkendall, *The United States, 1929–1945: Years of Crisis and Change* (New York: McGraw-Hill, 1973). Peter Fearon, *War, Prosperity and Depression: The U.S. Economy, 1917–45* (Oxford: Philip Allan, 1987), offers the approach of an economic historian. An influential essay on FDR (and another on Hoover) is to be found in Richard Hofstadter, *The American Political Tradition and the Men Who Made It* (New York: Knopf, 1948). A useful source of data is Patrick Renshaw, *America in the Era of the Two World Wars, 1910–1945* (Harlow: Longman, 1996).

William E. Leuchtenburg, *Franklin D. Roosevelt and the New Deal, 1932–1940* (New York: Harper & Row, 1963), remains one of the best introductions to the New Deal. An excellent topical approach, with chapters for example on labour and welfare, is Anthony J. Badger, *The New Deal: The Depression Years, 1933–1940* (Basingstoke: Macmillan, 1989), which also contains a very full bibliography. Brief general treatments of the United States in the war include Michael C.C. Adams, *The Best War Ever: America and World War II* (Baltimore: Johns Hopkins University Press, 1994), an ironic title, and Robert James Maddox, *The United States and*

World War II (Boulder and Oxford: Westview Press, 1992), which offers a helpful perspective by beginning with the First World War.

Specialised and thematic studies

A recent interpretative study of the whole of Roosevelt's presidency is Alan Brinkley, *The End of Reform: New Deal Liberalism in Recession and War* (New York: Knopf, 1995), and a thoughtful discussion beginning at an earlier date is Barry D. Karl, *The Uneasy State: The United States from 1915 to 1945* (Chicago: University of Chicago Press, 1983). Placing New Deal liberalism in longer perspective are the dated but lively Eric Goldman, *Rendezvous with Destiny: A History of Modern American Reform* (New York: Knopf, 1952), and the incisive Robert Harrison, *State and Society in Twentieth Century America* (London: Longman, 1997). A good collection of essays is Steve Fraser and Gary Gerstle, eds, *The Rise and Fall of the New Deal Order, 1930–1980* (Princeton: Princeton University Press, 1989).

On the Slump, see John Kenneth Galbraith, *The Great Crash, 1929* (London: Deutch, 3rd edn, 1973), and for a brief analysis Peter Fearon, *The Origins and Nature of the Great Slump, 1929–1932* (London: Macmillan, 1979). Robert S. McElvaine, *The Great Depression, 1929–1941* (New York: New York Times Books, 1984), is a vivid account. A wider view is taken in Dietmar Rothermund, *The Global Impact of The Great Crash, 1929–1939* (London: Routledge, 1996).

A pioneering and sympathetic study of the New Deal is Arthur M. Schlesinger Jr's trilogy of *The Age of Roosevelt* (Boston: Houghton Mifflin): *The Crisis of the Old Order* (1956), *The Coming of the New Deal* (1958) and *The Politics of Upheaval* (1960), though the story is not taken beyond 1936. The doyen of New Deal historians is William E. Leuchtenburg, whose introductory volume is cited above, but the serious student will want to consult his many other publications, such as the useful collection of essays entitled *The FDR Years: On Roosevelt and His Legacy* (New York: Columbia University Press, 1995) and his *The Supreme Court Reborn: Constitutional Revolution in the Age of Roosevelt* (New York: Oxford University Press, 1995). A major work on the New Deal and the economy is Ellis W. Hawley, *The New Deal and the Problem of Monopoly* (Princeton: Princeton University Press, 1966), and see also Albert U. Romasco, *The Politics of Recovery: Roosevelt's New Deal* (New York: Oxford University Press, 1983). Samuel Lubell, *The Future of American Politics* (New York: Harper & Row, 3rd edn, 1965), examines the development of the New Deal coalition, and excellent on the politics is John M. Allswang, *The New Deal and American Politics: A Study in Political Change* (New York: Wiley, 1978). On Roosevelt's populist opponents see Alan Brinkley, *Voices of Protest: Huey Long, Father Coughlin and the Great Depression* (New York: Knopf, 1982), and on Roosevelt's relationship with Capitol Hill see James T. Patterson, *Congressional Conservatism and the New Deal: The Growth of the Conservative Coalition in Congress, 1933–1939* (Lexington: University Press of Lexington, 1967). Nancy Weiss has examined the relationship of African Americans to the New Deal in *Farewell to the Party of Lincoln: Black Politics in the Age of FDR* (Princeton: Princeton University Press, 1983).

For perspectives from the left, see Paul K. Conkin, *The New Deal* (London: Routledge & Kegan Paul, 1968), and Barton J. Bernstein's essay in his edited volume *Towards a New Past: Dissenting Essays in American History* (New York: Pantheon, 1967). A recent analysis emphasising the pro-business (though often ineffective) policies of the New Deal is Colin Gordon, *New Deals: Business, Labor, and Politics in America, 1920–1935* (Cambridge: Cambridge University Press, 1994). An early conservative critique is Edgar Eugene Robinson, *The Roosevelt Leadership, 1933–1945* (Philadelphia: Lippincott, 1955).

The Roosevelt years embraced important episodes in labour history, on which see Robert H. Zieger, *American Workers, American Unions, 1920–1985* (Baltimore: Johns Hopkins University Press, 2nd edn, 1994), and Patrick Renshaw, *American Labour and Consensus Capitalism, 1935–1990* (Basingstoke: Macmillan, 1991). More detailed are Irving Bernstein, *The Lean Years: A History of the American Worker, 1920–1933* (Boston: Houghton Mifflin, 1960), and *The Turbulent Years: A History of the American Worker, 1933–41* (Boston: Houghton Mifflin, 1969). Specialised and important studies include Lizabeth Cohen, *Making a New Deal: Industrial Workers in Chicago, 1919–1939* (Cambridge: Cambridge University Press, 1990), Nelson Lichtenstein, *Labor's War at Home: The CIO in World War II* (Cambridge: Cambridge University Press, 1982), and, on the 1940s, Howell Harris, *The Right To Manage: Industrial Relations Policies of American Business* (Madison: University of Wisconsin Press, 1982).

Welfare history may be approached through Edward D. Berkowitz, *America's Welfare State from Roosevelt to Reagan* (Baltimore: Johns Hopkins University Press, 1991), and through James T. Patterson's studies, *America's Struggle Against Poverty, 1900–1985* (Cambridge MA: Harvard University Press, 2nd edn, 1986), and *The Welfare State in America, 1930–1980* (British Association for American Studies, 1981). Major contributions too are William R. Brock, *Welfare, Democracy and the New Deal* (Cambridge: Cambridge University Press, 1988), and Linda Gordon, *Pitied But Not Entitled: Single Mothers and the History of Welfare* (New York: Oxford University Press, 1994).

A lively and comprehensive general examination of the United States in the war is William L. O'Neill, *A Democracy at War: America's Fight at Home and Abroad in World War II* (Cambridge MA: Harvard University Press, 1993). Valuable studies focusing largely on the domestic impact of the war include Geoffrey Perrett, *Days of Sadness, Years of Triumph: The American People, 1939–1945* (Madison: University of Wisconsin Press, 1973), Richard Polenberg, *War and Society: The United States, 1941–1945* (Philadelphia: J. B. Lippincott, 1972), and John Morton Blum, *V Was For Victory: Politics and American Culture in World War II* (New York: Harcourt, Brace, Jovanovic, 1976). Harold G. Vatter offers an incisive economic analysis in *The U.S. Economy in World War II* (New York: Columbia University Press, 1985). Important aspects of domestic history are examined in Karen Anderson, *Wartime Women: Sex Roles, Family Relations, and the Status of Women in World War II* (Westport CT: Greenwood, 1981), Peter Irons, *Justice at War: The Inside Story of the Japanese-American Internment* (New York: Oxford University Press, 1983), and Neil A. Wynn, *The Afro-American and the Second World War* (London: Elek, 1976).

For long perspectives on foreign policy see Foster Rhea Dulles, *America's Rise to World Power, 1898–1954* (New York: Harper, 1955), and Robert H. Ferrell, *American Diplomacy: The Twentieth Century* (New York: Norton, 1988). An authoritative account of Roosevelt's foreign policy is Robert Dallek, *Franklin D. Roosevelt and American Foreign Policy, 1932–1945* (New York: Oxford University Press, 1979), and see also Frederick W. Marks III, *Wind Over Sand: The Diplomacy of Franklin Roosevelt* (Athens GA: The University of Georgia Press, 1987). Particular periods are examined in Wayne C. Cole, *Roosevelt and the Isolationists* (Lincoln: University of Nebraska Press, 1983), and Gaddis Smith, *American Diplomacy During the Second World War, 1941–1945* (New York: Knopf, 2nd edn, 1985). Also valuable are Warren F. Kimball, ed., *Franklin D. Roosevelt and the World Crisis, 1937–45* (Lexington MA: Heath, 1974), and Robert A. Divine, *Roosevelt and World War II* (Baltimore: Johns Hopkins University Press, 1969). A full account is Eric Larrabee, *Commander in Chief: Franklin Delano Roosevelt, His Lieutenants and Their War* (London: Deutsch, 1987). Good on the Pacific war is Ronald G. Spector, *Eagle Against the Sun: The American War with Japan* (New York: Vintage Books, 1985), and see also Akira Iriye, *Power and Culture: The Japanese-American War, 1941–1945* (Cambridge MA: Harvard University Press, 1981). On the Allied leadership see Herbert Feis, *Churchill, Roosevelt and Stalin: The War They Waged and The Peace They Sought* (Princeton: Princeton University Press, 1967), and Warren F. Kimball, ed., *Churchill and Roosevelt: The Complete Correspondence* (Princeton: Princeton University Press, 1984). An important study of a new kind of warfare is Michael S. Sherry, *The Rise of American Air Power: The Creation of Armageddon* (New Haven CT: Yale University Press, 1987). The roots of the Cold War have been located in the Second World War, as briefly discussed in Richard Crockatt, *The United States and the Origins of the Cold War, 1941–53* (BAAS Pamphlets in American Studies, 1990), and more substantially in John Lewis Gaddis, *The United States and the Origins of the Cold War, 1941–1947* (New York: Columbia University Press, 1972).

Franklin Roosevelt himself has been a problem for biographers, who seem to have found it difficult to treat him adequately in a single volume. The most ambitious account is unfinished, and will remain so, Frank Freidel's four volumes of *Franklin D. Roosevelt* (Boston: Little, Brown) taking the story to the summer of 1933: *The Apprenticeship* (1952), *The Ordeal* (1954), *The Triumph* (1956), and *Launching the New Deal* (1973). Perhaps the single most influential biographical analysis is James MacGregor Burns, *Roosevelt: The Lion and the Fox* (New York: Harcourt, Brace, 1956), supplemented by *Roosevelt: The Soldier of Freedom* (New York: Harbourt, Brace, 1970), focusing on foreign policy. A recent (often critical) biography is Patrick J. Maney, *The Roosevelt Presence: A Biography of FDR* (New York: Twayne, 1992), while Doris K. Goodwin examines a celebrated relationship in *No Ordinary Times: Franklin and Eleanor Roosevelt – The Home Front in World War II* (New York: Simon & Schuster, 1994). Important sources on Roosevelt are the memoirs of various New Dealers, including Frances Perkins, *The Roosevelt I Knew* (New York: Viking, 1946), Harold Ickes, *The Secret Diary of Harold L. Ickes, 1933–1941*, 3 vols (New York: Simon & Schuster, 1953–55), and David E. Lilienthal, *The Journals of David E. Lilienthal*, vol. I, 1939–45 (New York: Harper & Row, 1964).